modern cabin

modern cabin

NEW DESIGNS FOR AN AMERICAN ICON

MICHELLE KODIS

Gibbs Smith, Publisher

To enrich and inspire humankind

Salt Lake City | Charleston | Santa Fe | Santa Barbara

First Edition
11 10 09 08 07   5 4 3 2 1

Published by
Gibbs Smith, Publisher
P.O. Box 667
Layton, Utah 84041

Orders: 1.800.835.4993
www.gibbs-smith.com

Designed by Debra McQuiston
Printed and bound in China

Library of Congress Cataloging-in-Publication Data

Kodis, Michelle.
  Modern cabin: new designs for an American icon / Michelle Kodis.
— 1st ed.
      p. cm.
  ISBN-10: 1-4236-0099-1
  1. Vacation homes—United States—Designs and plans . 2. Architecture,
Domestic—United States—Designs and plans. I. Title.

NA8470.K63 2007
728.7'30973—dc22

2006033867

For Rich

Acknowledgments
The following individuals influenced this book, both directly and indirectly, and I am grateful for their guidance, input and support: Rich Cieciuch, Gibbs Smith, Suzanne Taylor, Christopher Robbins, Hollie Keith, Madge Baird, Carrie Westover, Anita Wood, Debra McQuiston, Rosemerry Wahtola Trommer, my lunch girls (Kierstin, Pam, Maureen), Marcia Cohen, Donna Fecteau, Susan Simpson, Kendall Cieciuch, and Andrew and Brett Cieciuch. Every book I write has to include a mention of my family and then of course my pal, Violet, without whom I would spend too many hours at the computer when I could be out taking a perfectly wonderful walk.

The photographs you see in this book come from an extraordinarily talented group of professionals. Without their images, my words would not have life.

As for the architects featured in these pages, my hope is that I have conveyed their work in a way that captures the true magnitude of their expertise and artistry.

contents

introduction

A number of years ago, my husband and I set off for a long weekend at a friend's mountain cabin. We packed a few days' worth of food, loaded the dogs into the back of the car and drove off, filled with the woozy anticipation of time away from the distractions and duties of everyday life. Still, in the interest of complete disclosure, in the backs of our minds we knew we wouldn't be completely isolated—after all, the cabin had phone service, which meant we could call in for work or other responsibilities, if needed. We would get away from it all, but not really.

Upon arriving at the quiet little cabin, reposed in a meadow resplendent with aspen trees ablaze in their autumn light show, we unpacked and sat on the porch to listen to the sparkling rush of a nearby river. My husband didn't sit for long, though—he had to make a phone call. I acquiesced: nothing wrong with that, it was important to check in, stay in touch. But the phone was not in agreement. There was no dial tone and no amount of wiggling the jack or repeatedly hanging up and picking up made any difference. Then we found a note from the owner explaining that the phones had been disconnected for the fall and winter seasons, when little activity was expected at the cabin. No worries, we had our cell phones. But each one stared back at us, blank-faced. No signal, not even a bleep. Both of us had trekked and

camped in the wilderness and had been on long river trips, far away from the conveniences of home, so we accepted our telecommunications-challenged fate and hunkered in. And in truth, it was the best thing for us. With no phones to distract and no e-mail to check, we had only each other for company—and our romping dogs and the deer and elk that spied on us from the lower meadow. We hiked the alpine trails, crusted with a wafer-thin layer of ice in the mornings, a sure sign of winter's approach, produced magical dinners from our no-fuss rations, and even popped in an old James Bond video. As we drove off several days later, I felt a palpable pull back to the cabin and the promise of its uncomplicated way of life. As we neared the highway, one of our cell phones gave a half-hearted bleat as its signal grew—even it sounded reluctant to come back to reality, having enjoyed its rest. I tell this story to illustrate what you already know—that getting away from it all is indeed a balm to the heart and soul. Like chocolate, we all love it but many of us don't allow ourselves nearly enough of it.

The first cabins in the United States were erected by settlers seeking protection from the elements and the ear-liest of those structures date back to the shelters constructed by Scandinavian pioneers near Wilmington, Delaware, in the seventeenth century. The untouched forests provided an abundant supply of wood for building and because of that cabins have come to represent a certain style: many are made from logs or feature wood as the dominant material. Since then the cabin has evolved into a true American icon, one that recalls simpler times. People are drawn to cabins because they represent a reprieve from busy life and offer the opportunity to connect with nature. The idea of a cozy cabin in the woods fills the overworked brain with visions of lazy days unburdened by demands and interruptions.

Despite its iconic stature, the cabin is no longer restrained by its origins. As you will discover in this book, the cabin has broken free of its history to become an entirely new kind of building. Yes, you will see logs and cabins that remind you of the images you may have cultivated in your mind over the years, but the designs in these pages are updated and tailored for contemporary life. Some of the cabins reveal ways to use ecologically sound materials and construction techniques while others take advantage of the money-saving benefits of prefabrication. Some are miles from a paved road and yet others are much closer to civilization. Some are vernacular and classic in appearance while others are modern masterpieces down to their tiniest details. Some are modest, others more spacious. What they all share is an undeniably current expression of the getaway house.

This book features twenty-two cabins organized into three sections: *Updated Rustic Charm*, *Beyond the Traditional Cabin*, and *Into the Future*. In *Updated Rustic Charm*, you'll find dwellings whose form and materiality refer to the cabin of the past but whose floor plans and materials are perfectly suited for today. The section titled *Beyond the Traditional Cabin* expands the concept of the present-day retreat with fresh ideas about architecture and construction, and *Into the Future* showcases ultramodern cabins constructed with cutting-edge building methods and materials.

My hope is that this book will give you many ideas to apply to your own cabin. Picture it: a place for contemplation, relaxation, having fun or doing absolutely nothing. Sounds divine, doesn't it?

updated
rustic charm

CABINS WITH A
TRADITIONAL
LOOK AND FEEL
BUT UPDATED
FOR TODAY'S
LIFESTYLES

The cabin is visible from the main house during the winter, as shown, but in the summer it disappears into the thick foliage of the trees. The architect placed new windows into the existing openings, a method that spared the expense of custom windows. Screened French doors open to the park-like setting.

the little cabin **that could**

DESIGN: GAR HARGENS, CLOSE ASSOCIATES

PHOTOGRAPHS: DON WONG

LOCATION: SHAFER, MINNESOTA   384 SQUARE FEET

This really is the story of the little cabin that could. Built by a couple who wanted to fine-tune their building techniques before embarking on the larger task of constructing their permanent home on a rural stretch of land near Shafer, Minnesota, the "practice cabin" was heading for ruin when architect Gar Hargens and his wife, Missy, discovered it while searching for a weekend getaway. The cabin had no electricity or plumbing and was in need of an exterior and interior facelift, but Hargens was motivated by the fact that the property had another, larger home on it and was only forty-five minutes from his primary residence in downtown St. Paul.

In its original state, the 384-square-foot cabin had potential, but its rough cedar siding and sagging windows needed replacing and inside it was about as close to roughing it as you can get without pitching a tent. Still, Hargens gladly accepted the task of remodeling the structure, despite the amount of work involved. "The sill beams were beginning to rot, and it was open in places and all of nature's creatures were getting to live there," he recalls.

SPECIAL FEATURES FOR THIS PLAN

- ICONIC CABIN FORM KEPT INTACT BUT MODERNIZED WITH LONG-LASTING MATERIALS AND SIMPLE CONVENIENCES
- ENVIRONMENTALLY-FRIENDLY COMPOSTING TOILET AND BASIC ELECTRICITY BUT NO PLUMBING

4

1 The roof is now tightly sealed against snow and rain.

2 A new entry addition was the only change to the cabin's footprint, and the architect used the trunk of a cedar tree to support the structure. Crisp white windows stand out against the red siding and, because white is a standard color, there was no extra expense involved in ordering a custom color.

3 The cabin is reminiscent of the farm buildings found throughout the region but has been given distinctly modern updates, including red metal siding and a silver metal roof.

The architect was careful to preserve the original form while transforming the structure from a near ruin into a usable space.

4 The cabin's steep gable roof was left intact but the original asphalt shingles were replaced with corrugated metal in a gleaming silver color, which serves as a dramatic contrast against the red siding. Although the metal roof and siding were not the least expensive materials in the architect's palette, thanks to their durability they will reveal their value over time.

"We realized in a hurry that we needed to get in there and fix this building before it was lost forever. We knew it would be worth the effort."

Working with a local contractor, Hargens drew up a plan for transforming the cabin into a functional outbuilding. He began by replacing the original concrete posts with a proper foundation. After that, he removed the board-and-batten siding, inspected it for rot, then cleaned and reinstalled it with the boards and battens placed side by side as the interior finish. The walls were covered with a structural insulated panel system (SIPS), which makes it possible to heat the entire space with just a small wood stove. In keeping with the region's agricultural vernacular, the cabin was given a fresh skin of long-lasting vertical red metal siding and topped with a galvanized metal roof in gleaming silver. A cedar tree trunk harvested from the land was used to support the entry canopy, where it serves as an organic contrast against the clean, straightforward lines of the siding and roof. Hargens made the cabin more livable by adding a composting toilet, wiring it for electricity, and creating a kitchen with microwave, under-counter refrigerator and counters and drop cabinets. He decided

against plumbing, figuring that bottled water would suit the casual use of the building just fine.

In addition to its metal siding and roof, the cabin has been updated with crisp white windows in standard sizes that fit neatly into the original openings (this technique avoided the higher costs associated with custom sizes). Bead board in a vertical and horizontal pattern imparts a contemporary look to the entry, which complements the less-refined styling of the main space. Hargens added another loft to increase the usable square footage of the cabin, and linoleum and oak plywood flooring took it from down-in-the-dumps to warm and inviting.

"The cabin still has a traditional, classic look inside, and on the outside it reflects the local agrarian buildings but in a streamlined and modern way," Hargens points out. "That, combined with the tranquil setting and the short driving distance, has made this place our dream retreat."

5 The structural beams of the loft are connected by classic scarf joints, which impart a traditional look to the interior.

6 The remodel of the cabin involved the installation of a structural insulated panel system (SIPS), an excellent choice for cold climates.

7 The kitchen/dining area occupies one end of the cabin. The flooring is economical oak plywood held down with exposed screws.

8 The cabin has two lofts, each with a drop-down stair and a steel railing canted at the midpoint to resemble a hayloft rail. The ceiling is twenty-five feet high at the ridgeline, and the ceiling beams are oak. The wallboards were salvaged from the original exterior siding.

9 Although the main space of the cabin is open, the lofts provide areas of privacy and are intimate in scale.

10 The entry addition features a linoleum floor and horizontal and vertical bead board, a more finished and refined complement to the rustic main room. The bathroom has been outfitted with a composting toilet.

7

The classic look combined with the tranquil setting has made this place our dream retreat.

8

9

10

The setting is quintessentially Western: a grassy meadow, mountains in the distance and even a river running through the property. The house sits low to the ground, resting gently on the site rather than attempting to take it over.

at home in **the meadow**

DESIGN: CARNEY ARCHITECTS
PHOTOGRAPHS: PAUL WARCHOL
LOCATION: PINEDALE, WYOMING   3,700 SQUARE FEET

Carney Architects' goal for this Wyoming retreat was to create a home that would respect the state's ranching history while making a definitive break from tradition to reveal a contemporary façade and a truly up-to-date arrangement of living space.

The owners, retirees from Chicago with a passion for the outdoors, brought "sophisticated taste and the desiré for a home appropriate to the setting and locale, but they didn't have preconceived notions of how the building should look," says Eric Logan, a member of the team that worked on the house. While the clients did express interest in finding a way to incorporate logs into the design, judging from the result they clearly did not issue a mandate for a traditional log cabin. Instead, Logan says, the objective was to find ways to push the boundaries of the typical Western house. In other words, this house was to become something that would stand apart from the many log homes found in nearby Jackson and throughout the region.

SPECIAL FEATURES FOR THIS PLAN

- RECOGNIZES THE REGION'S RANCH BUILDINGS WHILE SHOWCASING THE BEAUTY OF CONTEMPORARY FORMS AND MATERIALS

- COLLECTION OF SMALL SEPARATE BUILDINGS ORGANIZED ALONG A LOG WALL, A PLAN THAT OFFERS EASY CIRCULATION THROUGH THE INTERIORS AND CLEARLY INDICATES PUBLIC AND PRIVATE ZONES

1 The low-slung building is composed of three shed-roof pavilions linked with a log wall. The sheds resemble the agricultural structures found throughout the region but their styling and materiality speak a contemporary language. The individual pavilions also provide separation between the home's public and private zones. Exterior materials include treated cedar siding, field stone, oxidized steel panels (on the projection at the master bathroom pavilion, to the right) and square-cut logs.

Those spoken goals morphed into a physical reality as the architectural team began to sketch out the placement of and interaction between the home's main components: three low-slung shed volumes, or pavilions, that stretch the building across the site, minimizing the scale of the composition and in turn creating more comfortable and intimate living spaces. From a functional perspective, the pavilions divide the house into discrete public and private zones: a living/dining/ kitchen great room, a combined garage/guest room/entry, and a master suite/office. Each of the pavilions is positioned to maximize interior ambient light and capture the see-forever views. The architects also paid attention to the importance of creating livable spaces outdoors—to that end, they arranged the pavilions to form a partially enclosed courtyard. In this manner, the house wraps around itself, facing the views in all outward directions and turning inward at its core.

Understandably, the grand views exerted a significant influence on how the building was worked into its setting. Its exterior materials purposely understated, the home hunkers down into the landscape of rye grass and willow and cottonwood trees punctuated by marshy wetlands and the North Fork River, which runs through the property. The Wind River Mountains in the distance are expertly framed by large windows kept free of coverings—plenty of space around the house and no neighbors within sight omitted the need for privacy-enhancing measures.

Responding to the clients' request for a minimal infusion of the traditional, the architects oriented the pavilions along a wall constructed of sturdy square-cut logs. This "spine" provided the opportunity to "turn the logs into something special," Logan explains. The wall serves as an organizer for the interior spaces, but it doesn't stop there: it continues inside, where it forms one side of a semi-enclosed terrace off the great room. "The wall ended up becoming a key part of the house and, because it guides circulation through the rooms, it acts as a kind of anchor in the space," Logan adds.

The home has another anchor: a sturdy stone chimney intersected by the roof of the great room pavilion. The architects, proponents of exposing the bones of a building rather than covering them up, made the structure of this house integral to its overall scheme. "Exposed structures are like built-in decorative elements," Logan points out. "You don't have to add anything— it's already there." This technique is evident outside, in the tilted roof structure, and inside on certain portions of the ceiling.

Materials were pared down and selected for their ability to keep the house as inconspicuous as possible; in addition to the logs, they include cedar siding, oxidized steel panels, fieldstone, rusted corrugated metal and concrete. The interiors were directed by John and Nina Hancock, a husband-and-wife design team from Chicago. The Hancocks not only selected fabrics and furnishings but in some cases oversaw the creation of custom pieces such as headboards, bedside tables and end tables.

2   A hefty stone chimney at the corner of the great room helps ground the building and is a structural stabilizer. The roof extends beyond the pavilion to form a covered seating terrace, a technique that enhances the home's indoor/outdoor connection, keeping it in constant dialogue with the landscape. The architects chose to leave certain areas of the building, such as the roof, exposed, which not only reduced costs but allowed the infrastructure of the home to become a decorative accent. The log wall extends beyond the building to partially enclose the terrace.

3, 4

3 The home's fenestration frames near and distant views, creating pockets of intimacy where needed, such as at the master bedroom pavilion, and opening up the house to the wide vistas elsewhere. The roof is rusted corrugated metal, a material suitable for the sometimes harsh Wyoming weather and yet another nod to the region's agricultural roots. The cedar siding has been stained to prevent graying and the windows, which pop out of the walls, are clad in rusted metal.

4 A wall of square-cut, kiln-dried logs starts at the entry and continues inside, where it becomes the "spine" of the house, organizing the individual pavilions and directing circulation through the interiors. Rainwater is funneled into the courtyard by a thin steel scupper, and the decks are untreated cedar.

Terrace

Great Room

5 The log spine separates the main living pavilion from the courtyard. Square-cut logs used in a limited application provided the rustic look the owners wanted without turning the building into a log cabin.

6 The great room pavilion has a vaulted ceiling with exposed trusses, while the other two pavilions have lower, more intimate ceilings. The architects and interior designers opted for warm interior finishes to instill an inviting, casual ambience. Materials include a blackened steel panel on the kitchen island and concrete flooring with radiant in-floor heat. The overall look is one of refined rusticity.

7 The hallway off the main entry is a comfortable place to sit and remove or put on shoes. To the right, a sliding fir door on barn-style track hardware closes off the powder room. The back wall is clad in blackened steel panels, which bring an industrial element to the décor.

8 Large windows in the great room provide unimpeded views of the distant Wind River Mountains, and the smaller windows can be opened to allow cooling breezes to move through the room. The stone fireplace at the corner visually anchors the glass-filled space. The custom dining table is by David Trapp of Victor, Idaho.

9 With its low fir ceiling and narrow windows, the master bedroom pavilion is more intimately scaled than the great room, and its subdued textures and colors—a gray fabric panel behind the bed and pale yellow walls—impart a tranquil mood.

10 The master bath features painted wood cabinets and a frameless glass steam shower enclosure.

lily pad cabin

DESIGN: MATTHEW ACKERMAN, CATALYST ARCHITECTURE
PHOTOGRAPHS: MATTHEW ACKERMAN AND MICHAEL FRENCH
LOCATION: LAKE HORSE SHOE BEND, TEXAS   1,050 SQUARE FEET

yrically named the Lily Pad Cabin, this small getaway in the piney woods of east Texas is intended to remind the owners of their days spent camping on the site before commissioning their permanent shelter. "The clients wanted a comfortable yet unpretentious vacation home with a very intimate interaction with the outdoors, similar to what they had experienced sleeping in a tent," says Matthew Ackerman, the architect hired to design the cabin, which sits on two acres of land on the shores of Lake Horse Shoe Bend.

The cabin is just 1,050 square feet in size but its open floor plan and the absence of full interior walls make it appear more spacious. The clients were specific about what they wanted in their retreat: a round house with 360-degree views; lots of windows; hardwood floors; a wraparound deck to "blur the boundary between inside and out"; and a wood-burning fireplace. And there was another requirement: it had to be as inexpensive as possible.

Ackerman accentuated the cabin's rusticity by leaving the roof framing exposed to the interior and by using Western red cedar throughout the building. The round shape was achieved with a twelve-faceted wall system that created the opportunity for extensive glazing to maximize the forest views. The undulating roof—the inspiration for the Lily Pad moniker—relied on an innovative framing technique that resulted in an up-and-down motion to the perimeter bearing walls, which in turn brought "an organic rippling effect to the exterior roofline that echoes the lily pads found along the edges of the lake," the architect points out.

SPECIAL FEATURES FOR THIS PLAN

- UNDULATING ROOF FORM REMINISCENT OF THE LILY PADS ON A NEARBY LAKE

- CIRCULAR OPEN FLOOR PLAN WITH MINIMAL INTERIOR WALL DIVISIONS

- INTRICATE, ONE-OF-A-KIND DESIGN ACHIEVED ON A LIMITED BUDGET

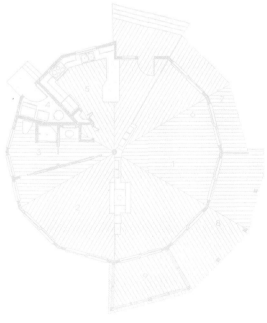

Despite the intricacy of the roof form, Ackerman was able to bring the budget in at about $72 per square foot, a more-than-reasonable price for a building that moves far beyond the definition of a conventional cabin in the woods.

The house opens to its setting through commercial-sized sliding glass doors that provide easy access to the 450-square-foot covered wraparound deck and the lake beyond. The region's dramatic weather fluctuations—scorching in the summer, freezing in the winter—made the task of adequate ventilation and efficient heating key aspects of the design. Ackerman extended the roof overhangs to let in just the right amount of sunshine and installed an

electrical skylight that vents hot air through the roof—crucial in the summer. When temperatures drop, a double-sided wood-burning fireplace, positioned as a central element in the room, heats the entire space. The fireplace divides the living/dining area and the bedroom, which is located behind a half-wall that screens the bed from the main space without blocking the views or interfering with the natural light that pours into the cabin.

In addition to the cedar used on the building, Ackerman used finish-grade stained plywood for the kitchen counters and tongue-and-groove pine for the ceiling and floor, materials that give the interior the rustic but minimalist look the owners wanted.

"The Lily Pad's style is contemporary and welcoming," Ackerman says. "It reflects the mood of the site itself—that of quiet warmth. And, even inside the structure, you almost feel as if you're camping out."

1 The cabin's innovative roof design resulted in an undulating form reminiscent of the lily pads that skim the surface of a nearby lake. Although rustic in appearance, the cabin features contemporary styling inside and is equipped with the conveniences of home. The open floor plan connects to a screened porch that extends into the forest, enhancing the building's connection to the two-acre site. Photo by Michael French.

2 The owners requested a simple kitchen with open shelving to help keep the space light and airy. The cabinets and counters were crafted from finish-grade stained plywood with a polyurethane coating. Photo by Matthew Ackerman.

2 The architect chose Western red cedar for the cabin exterior because of its durability and stained it to prevent it from graying under exposure to the elements. The deck is pine. Photo by Matthew Ackerman.

3

4   The complexity of the roof structure is visible inside the cabin. An untreated telephone pole became the building's key structural element—and it cost just $125. Photo by Matthew Ackerman.

5   Large commercial sliding glass doors on six of the building's twelve facets impart a transparency to the cabin—important to the owners, who wanted an intimate connection to the outdoors while remaining sheltered inside. The floors are stained pine. Photo by Matthew Ackerman.

6   The cabin's open layout reveals a spaciousness that belies the 1,050-square-foot plan. The architect avoided full walls, opting instead for one low wall that separates the sleeping area from the living/dining room. An electrical skylight performs double duty by increasing ambient light and venting hot air through the roof in the summer. The cabin's dramatic roof structure is mimicked inside with a ceiling clad in tongue-and-groove pine. The twin vertical elements—the center post and the exposed flue—refer to the many trees on the site. Photo by Matthew Ackerman.

7   Finding a place for everything is important in any small space. Here, an opening in the half-wall became the perfect place for a built-in shelf. Photo by Matthew Ackerman.

The post-and-beam building retained its character even after a meticulous reconstruction that involved adding a cedar shingle roof, wood siding, thick insulation, and ample glazing that acts as a passive-solar device to warm the interiors, particularly important during the region's cold winters. The stained-fir windows also provide cross ventilation when the mercury rises.

new life for a salvaged **building**

DESIGN: CANDACE TILLOTSON-MILLER

PHOTOGRAPHS: ROGER WADE

LOCATION: SUN VALLEY, IDAHO   900 SQUARE FEET

Merging old with new can be a daunting prospect, but architect Candace Tillotson-Miller was successful in her efforts to transform a dilapidated post-and-beam barn into a habitable, light-filled retreat/art studio for a Sun Valley couple with modern taste and a love for traditional structures.

The nineteenth-century barn was shipped from Vermont under the guidance of a cabin broker and then rebuilt according to a design by Tillotson-Miller. Her challenge, she reveals, was to reinvent the building while staying true to its original framework and without sacrificing its authenticity. Also key was orienting the house to capture as much natural light as possible—important to one of the owners, an artist—and maximizing the views in all directions while ensuring privacy. Although the setting appears to be acres of open, rolling hills, its location is a subdivision peppered with neighboring houses.

"We kept the building understated but gave it a degree of elegance and refinement that we knew wouldn't overwhelm its simplicity," the architect says. "Barns tend to be large in terms of their massing, and while it's true that living in a barn is appealing to many people, you have to be careful to maintain the proper scale, otherwise it just won't feel right."

UPDATED RUSTIC CHARM 40 NEW LIFE FOR A SALVAGED BUILDING

SPECIAL FEATURES FOR THIS PLAN

- OLD POST-AND-BEAM BARN TRANSFORMED INTO A RETREAT/ART STUDIO WITH CLEAN LINES AND STRONG TIES TO THE PAST

- RESEMBLES A RURAL FARM BUILDING BUT IN REALITY IS LOCATED IN AN ACTIVE SUBDIVISION

At 900 square feet, this retreat does feel intimate and comfortable but ample windows, which open the interior to the landscape and fill the rooms with light, create the illusion of a larger space. The windows, in fact, became integral to the design, Tillotson-Miller explains, pointing out that they were "placed in a way that showed respect for the building—it was all about honoring the old barn. We didn't want to forget that during the process."

The barn arrived in pieces, its posts and beams disassembled and then laid out for reconstruction. Wood from a different barn was used to sheath the exterior and the building received a new cedar shingle roof. Inside, an open floor plan accommodates a great room with a small kitchenette. The building's twenty-eight-foot ceiling made it possible to add a loft over the main living area; the loft houses a bedroom and bathroom, as well as a small art studio. The interior materials were kept as minimal as possible to allow the natural beauty of wood to take the spotlight, and a concrete floor with radiant in-floor heat keeps the interiors cozy even during the cold mountain winters.

1 The 900-square-foot barn efficiently combines living space with a storage room, located behind a set of wood doors.

2 The ladder leading to the loft was part of the salvaged barn; the architect cleaned it up and incorporated it into the new design. The windows frame the pastoral views and in some places can be opened to ventilate the rooms.

3 The minimalist kitchen features custom fir cabinetry, a soapstone sink and counters, and contemporary light fixtures.

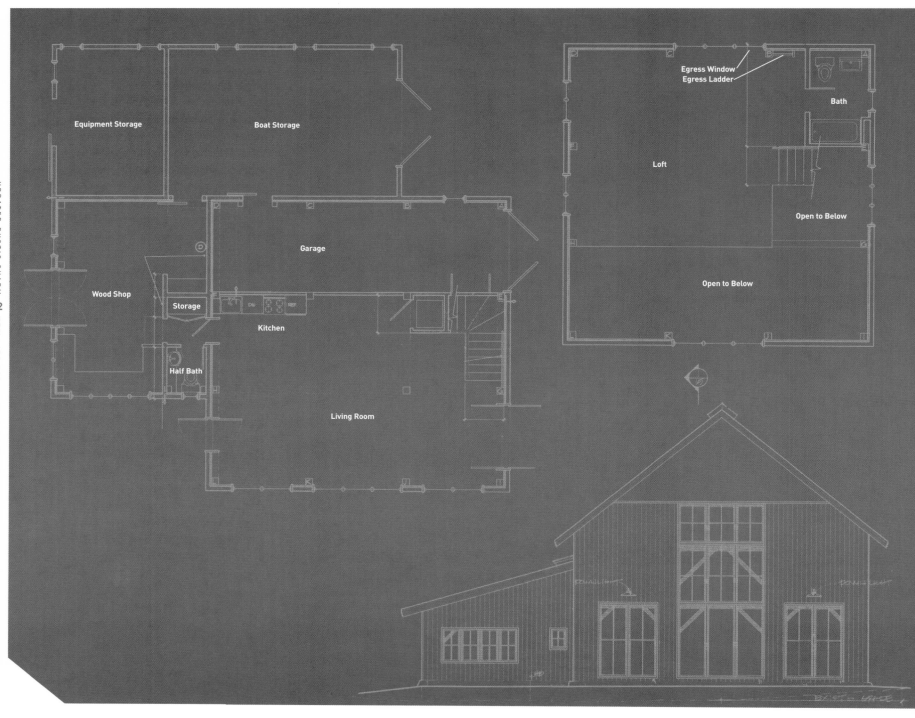

Equipment Storage

Boat Storage

Egress Window
Egress Ladder

Bath

Loft

Open to Below

Wood Shop

Garage

Open to Below

Storage

Kitchen

Half Bath

Living Room

4 The rusticity of the exterior continues inside, where rough beams and wall boards complement the smooth concrete floor and painted stair. A narrow clerestory window welcomes sunlight.

5 The bathroom is tucked into a corner of the building.

6 The horizontal beam above the bed can be used as a shelf, and the ladder, originally the barn's hayloft access, now serves as a decorative element.

Cedar Shingle Roof

Corrugated Black Metal Roof

Aged & Rough-Sawn Random Width Boards

Applied Stone Veneer

The interior materials were kept as minimal as possible to allow the beauty of the wood to take the spotlight.

7   The owner added a splash of color to the otherwise mono-chromatic palette by staining a square of the loft floor a cheerful pumpkin and, for con-trast, bordering it with a strip of natural fir. The twenty-eight-foot-high ceiling adds drama to the space but careful attention paid to the scaling of the rooms ensured that the living areas would remain intimate.

8   The architect took advantage of the high ceiling to create a light-filled great room that includes a kitchenette and loft. Concrete floors with radiant in-floor heat work in tandem with the windows to keep the rooms at a comfortable temperature.

8

The cabin is located near Lake Travis, approximately twenty-five miles from Austin. The arrangement of the three individual cabins, as well as the care taken to preserve the character of the reclaimed materials, resulted in a home that looks as if it has stood for many years in its current configuration.

three reclaimed cabins **become one**

DESIGN: CHARLES TRAVIS

PHOTOGRAPHS: PAUL BARDAGJY

LOCATION: SPICEWOOD, TEXAS   1,800 SQUARE FEET

Plenty of cabins have been restored or remodeled, but this home in Spicewood, Texas, has an unusual story: it consists of three reclaimed cabins that were disassembled, trucked in from three different locations, and rebuilt on the site.

Architect Charles Travis, who oversaw the project, says the challenge was to incorporate new construction in and around the original cabin forms without sacrificing their character. "The whole thing was a good idea from the get-go, but for this to be a success, the cabins needed to be distinct, not covered up or disguised, and remain individual within the composition of the building," he explains.

Working closely with owner Gloria Frame, an interior designer, Travis found a solution: allow the cabins to stand as single entities but connect them with short breezeways. The breezeways link the larger main center cabin (living room) with the two smaller cabins on either side (the kitchen and bedrooms, respectively). This arrangement of space made it possible to divide the cabins into living areas with clearly defined functions, and the result is an 1,800-square-foot home with a seamless integration of old and new, and which maintains its ties to the past even as it reveals subtle contemporary accents.

SPECIAL FEATURES FOR THIS PLAN

- RESOURCEFUL BUILDING PROGRAM THAT COMBINED THREE SEPARATE CABINS INTO A WEEKEND RETREAT

- METICULOUS BLENDING OF OLD AND NEW IN ORDER TO RETAIN THE LOOK OF THE CABINS WHILE CREATING A LIVABLE STRUCTURE SUITED TO CONTEMPORARY LIFE

3

exposed. And he purposely did not alter the width or size of the cabins, nor did he change their scale.

After rebuilding the cabins with the help of a contractor specially trained in working with reclaimed structures, Travis had to make them livable. He cut openings for windows and doors and chinked the logs inside and out to seal the walls. Each cabin was capped with a galvanized metal roof, and small shed-roof additions at the kitchen and bedroom cabins neatly expanded the living space. The main cabin got a front porch and a large screened porch/outdoor living room off the back. Inside, the spaces flow together in a series of successive openings, a straightforward way to connect the three forms and create a strong visual line between them.

Travis and his client are thrilled with the outcome—and the fact that the entire process took less than a year. Beyond that, though, the architect derived a great deal of satisfaction from knowing that he had preserved a bit of history. "There is an authenticity to this house that you can just feel," Travis says, "and in many ways it became a celebration of materials that still had life in them."

1 The cabins' distinct rooflines rise above shed-roof additions clad in stone veneer. The additions expanded the living space without altering the footprint of the original structures. The main cabin is flanked by the kitchen cabin to the left and the bedroom cabin to the right, and gabled breezeways provide clear transitions between the spaces.

2 Clerestory windows in the living room cabin, the largest of the three, allow the room to fill with light. The flooring is reclaimed wood planks finished with a dark stain.

3 The spacious kitchen cabin features a Pennsylvania bluestone floor, stainless steel counters and a white ceiling that serves as a visual contrast against the dark timbers.

Although the disassembled cabins' logs and framing materials were in a dismal state when they arrived on the site ("What I saw was pretty scary," Travis acknowledges. "Some of the timbers were in bad shape, and it was hard to visualize how it would work out."), they were sturdy enough for the architect to be able to see beyond his initial impression. The authentic rusticity of the materials turned out to be integral to the overall design of the home. Wherever possible, Travis left the timbers and framing elements

4 The cabins were shored up with stone walls and "pop out" additions to increase living space. The timbers, which were left intact, are visible on both the exterior and interior.

5 Easily accessed from both breezeways, the screened porch is designed to look and feel like an outdoor living room. The architect installed built-in beds on each side of the wood-burning fireplace to provide extra sleeping space for guests. Materials include weathered limestone on the fireplace, reclaimed wood planks and rafters on the ceiling, and a stained cedar floor.

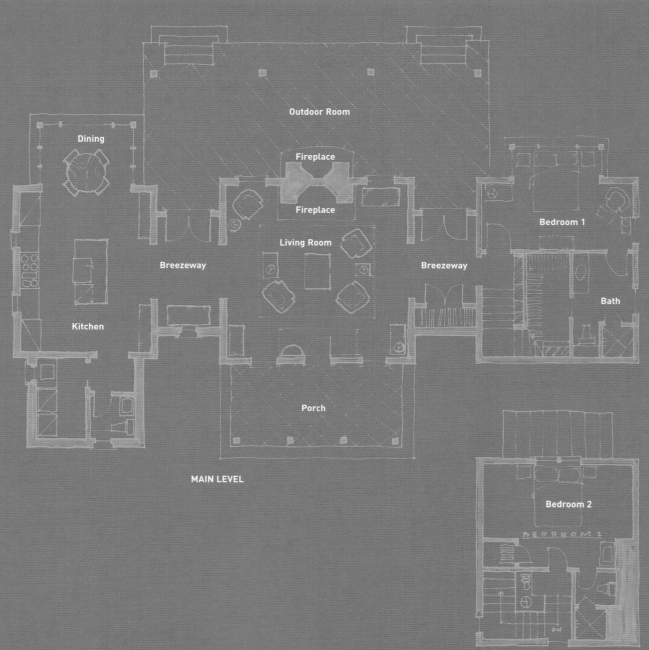

Outdoor Room

Dining

Fireplace

Fireplace

Bedroom 1

Living Room

Breezeway

Breezeway

Bath

Kitchen

Porch

MAIN LEVEL

Bedroom 2

UPPER LEVEL

6

6 The master bedroom, located on the lower floor of the bedroom cabin, reveals the successful merging of yesterday and today: heavy timbers and bold chinking refer to the past, while a bay window in the alcove addition brings the house into a new era.

7 The master bathroom, which is minimal in scale and pared-down in its detailing, has plaster walls finished with a custom tint made by the owner, an interior designer: she blended instant coffee into the plaster to create an aged, warm patina. The vanity was crafted from forged iron and the floor tiles are travertine.

8 Left exposed wherever possible, the rustic timbers became the principal interior design element. This is particularly evident in the living room, where the chinked logs bring a strong horizontality to the space.

7

Large south-facing windows at the great room provide views of the coastline, maximize natural light inside the building and ventilate the rooms. The high-performance low-e windows are argon-filled to minimize heat loss during the cooler months. The stepped-down roof accommodates a vegetative roof at the upper level and photovoltaic panels on the lower, which also serves as a cover for the patio. Photo by Greg Kozawa.

eco-friendly beach **retreat**

DESIGN: NATHAN GOOD

PHOTOGRAPHS: GREG KOZAWA AND NATHAN GOOD

LOCATION: CANNON BEACH, OREGON   2,268 SQUARE FEET

Here's something any homeowner would love to see: an electricity meter that every now and then takes an unusual turn and begins to spin backwards, crediting for energy use instead of clocking up the charges every month.

That is exactly what happens in the "net-zero-energy" home designed by architect Nathan Good for a couple with a proven commitment to treading lightly (their business headquarters was one of the first green commercial buildings in Oregon). Net-zero-energy describes a building that produces as much, or in some cases more, electricity as it consumes, but Good went a step further by taking the house toward a "carbon neutral" status—in other words, making sure that it relied very little on the energy supplied by fossil fuels.

In addition to the required eco-friendly features, Good's clients wanted a modestly sized, comfortable retreat that would last for generations and not require a lot of maintenance. He responded with a plan for a 2,268-square-foot structure that nestles into its hillside setting, where it overlooks spectacular views of the Oregon coastline. Southern exposure, an open floor plan with a minimal number of interior walls and a band of clerestory windows together bring as much natural light into the house as possible, even on overcast days.

SPECIAL FEATURES FOR THIS PLAN

- GENERATES AS MUCH ENERGY AS IT CONSUMES THANKS TO AN INNOVATIVE SOLAR/THERMAL POWER SYSTEM

- ECO-CONSCIOUS MATERIALS AND TECHNIQUES: WIND-FALLEN CEDAR; SUSTAINABLY GROWN WOOD FOR FLOORS, FRAMING AND CABINETRY; SALVAGED DOORS, HARDWARE AND BATHROOM FIXTURES; AND AN INSULATING VEGETATIVE ROOF

The form of the building revolves around two interlocking curved roofs (Good found his inspiration while studying photographs of sand dunes). This stepped-down design nimbly met the goal of combining a pleasing aesthetic with practicality. For the purposes of beauty, the upper roof was turned into a vegetative roof with flowering perennials; this gives the uphill neighbors a pleasant view of greenery instead of a solid mass of materials. Beyond its visual appeal, though, the roof is low maintenance, will last for fifty-plus years, is an excellent insulator, is fire-resistant and reduces storm-water run-off—important in this locale, where annual rainfall averages ninety inches.

The lower roof performs double duty as a platform for a series of low-profile photovoltaic panels and shelter for the patio below. The PV panels are hooked up to the neighborhood electrical grid and, if the house generates more electricity than it's consuming, the meter spins backwards, in the process lowering the owners' energy costs. And it gets better: any excess energy returns to a residential-scale electrical power plant. The home's heat and hot water are provided by a combined system of solar-thermal collectors, a ground-source heating pump, and energy recovery ventilators, Good explains.

Staying true to the home's environmentally conscious qualities, Good selected Forest Stewardship Council (FSC)–certified lumber for the interior wall framing and roof structure, support columns and cabinets. Wind-fallen trees were turned into heavy-timber framing inside, as well as flooring and a stair, and Douglas fir logs pulled from the Columbia River were crafted into interior doors and trim. Good's clients also found salvaged doors, appliances and bath fixtures.

Other green materials include rot- and pest-resistant Durisol insulating concrete forms for exterior walls; the forms have concrete cores mixed with fly ash, a waste material generated by coal-fired power plants. This house was one of the first in the region to use the product.

While it's true that Good's clients spent more money up front to save money later, their efforts illustrate that building a home can become an exercise in giving back to the planet.

"The clients pushed us every step of the way," Good says. "It was a dynamic and exciting process, figuring out how to make this house as green and sustainable as possible while simultaneously giving it a character that would reflect the owners' interest in the shapes, colors and textures found in nature."

1 Covered in flowering perennials, the vegetative roof serves a number of purposes: it softens the uphill neighbor's view, will last for decades, is fire-resistant and reduces storm-water runoff. Although the roof cost approximately 20 percent more than a conventional standing seam metal roof, it will last twice as long. Photo by Nathan Good.

2 Plaster walls and a Douglas fir floor complement the basalt stone used in the great room. The stone retains heat from the sun, operating like a solar flywheel and in turn helping to warm the room and reduce energy costs even further. The arches are wind-fallen cedar. Photo by Greg Kozawa.

3 The kitchen is located in the great room but positioned under the loft to give it a feeling of enclosure. The heavy-timber framing for the loft was milled from wind-fallen Douglas fir logs. The cabinets and island are FSC-certified cherry, and the counters are granite. Photo by Nathan Good.

4 The home is a virtual electricity-generating machine. Photovoltaic panels on the lower roof are hooked up to the neighborhood's electrical grid, and when the home produces more electricity than it uses, the meter spins backwards, giving the owners credits toward their utility bills. Photo by Nathan Good.

5 Solar-thermal collectors on the south-facing slope below the house harness solar energy to heat water in a circulating loop. A heat exchanger then transfers the heat from the loop to two 120-gallon storage tanks located in the basement, thus providing hot water for the house. Any excess heat is stored in the basalt-rock formations under the house, where it can be extracted as needed by a ground-source heat pump. Photo by Nathan Good.

SECTION THRU GREATROOM

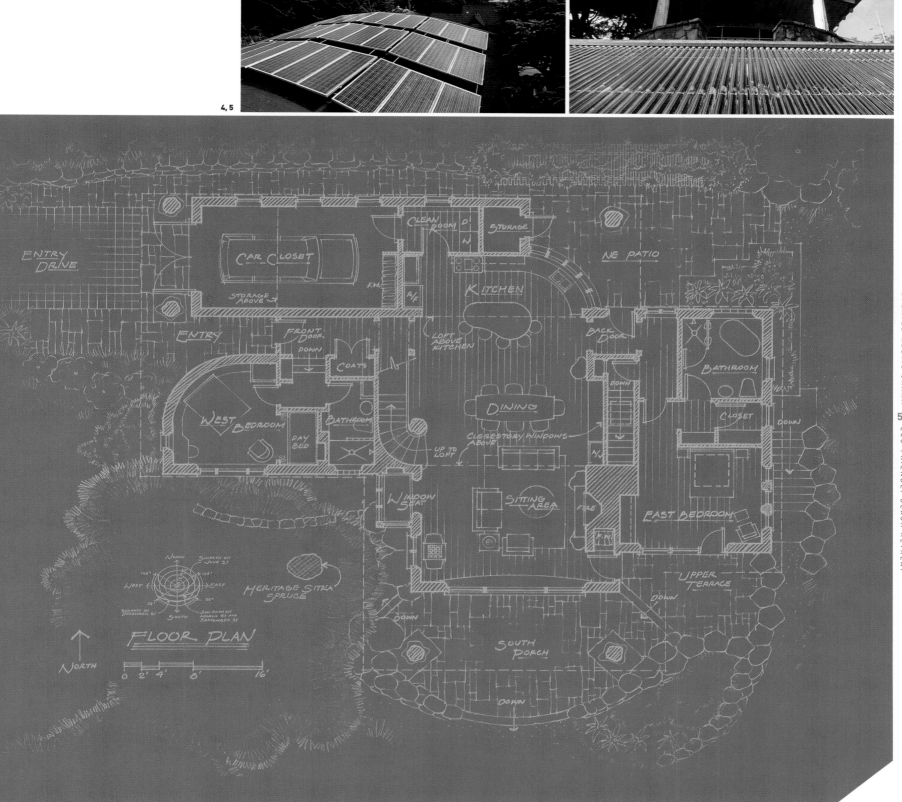

4, 5

ENTRY
DRIVE

CAR CLOSET

STORAGE ABOVE

CLEAN ROOM D/W

STORAGE

NE PATIO

KITCHEN

R/W

R/F

ENTRY

FRONT DOOR

DOWN

COATS

LOFT ABOVE KITCHEN

BACK DOOR

BATHROOM

WEST BEDROOM

DAY BED

BATHROOM

DINING

DOWN

CLOSET

DOWN

UP TO LOFT

CLERESTORY WINDOWS ABOVE

WINDOW SEAT

SITTING AREA

FIRE

EAST BEDROOM

NORTH

SUN PATH ON JUNE 21

104°

104°

WEST

EAST

66°

66°

SUN PATH ON DECEMBER 21

SOUTH

SUN PATH ON MARCH 21 AND SEPTEMBER 21

HERITAGE SITKA SPRUCE

UPPER TERRACE

DOWN

FLOOR PLAN

NORTH

0 2' 4'   8'   16'

SOUTH PORCH

DOWN

DOWN

It was a dynamic and exciting process, figuring out how to make this house as green and sustainable as possible while giving it a character that would reflect the owners' interest in the shapes, colors and textures found in nature.

6 The master bedroom opens to a private deck on the upper roof. The ceiling is tongue-and-groove pine and the floors are Douglas fir. Photo by Nathan Good.

7 The stair to the loft features a curving steel handrail that wraps around a windfallen incense-cedar trunk support, Douglas fir treads and a stone slab at the base. The rock to the right of the trunk was left over during construction of the fireplace, and rather than take on the difficult task of moving it outdoors, the owners decided to leave it in the house. A band of clerestory windows above the stair welcomes sunlight into the space, imbuing the interiors with a soft glow. Photo by Greg Kozawa.

8 The loft contains a guest bedroom and home office, and its proximity to the great room facilitates easy communication between people in the house. Healthy interior materials, paints, stains and sealants won't offgas volatile organic compounds (VOCs) and urea-formaldehyde. Photo by Nathan Good.

9 A glass block wall in the master bathroom allows light in while ensuring privacy. Plaster walls and slate tile brought the simple but warm look the owners wanted. A tile artisan created the pebble pattern on the floor, which is intended to look like sea foam washing up on the beach. Photo by Greg Kozawa.

7

8

9

traditional outside, **modern inside**

DESIGN: ARCHIMANIA

PHOTOGRAPHS: MAXWELL MACKENZIE

LOCATION: FLINT HILL, VIRGINIA   900 SQUARE FEET

First, a disclaimer: this small building in the rolling hills of rural Virginia is used as a pool house, which technically means it is not a cabin. But it qualified for this book because its design and layout could be readily adapted to a more cabin-like setting. Its no-fuss façade will appeal to those looking to build a retreat with architectural references to the past but constructed with contemporary materials that will last for years with minimal maintenance.

Todd Walker, working with a project team at Archimania, designed the house for a client from Washington, D.C., who "became infatuated with the old buildings in the area," he explains. "He would send me photos of these wonderful houses, which had great scale and proportion and looked appropriate in the countryside."

Archimania's client requested a straightforward program with no unnecessary finishes, and the architects' response was spot-on: an unquestionably current interpretation of the farm structures common to the area. Archimania, known and awarded in the profession for their exaggerated lines, striking angles and liberal use of color, admittedly did have to rein themselves in somewhat with this job, but that didn't prevent them from expressing a unique style. The building, a companion to a larger home on the site that Archimania renovated, is a tall, narrow box capped with a steeply pitched metal roof that stops short of forming an eave. Crisp, precise lines and a

SPECIAL FEATURES FOR THIS PLAN

- MODELED AFTER TRADITIONAL FARM STRUCTURES BUT CONSTRUCTED WITH MODERN MATERIALS THAT EMPHASIZE THE BEAUTY OF A CLEAN, SOPHISTICATED DESIGN

- FLEXIBLE FLOOR PLAN THAT CONTAINS VARIOUS FUNCTIONS WITHIN A STREAMLINED 900 SQUARE FEET

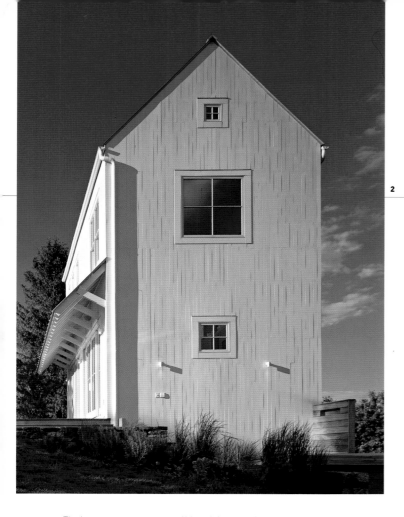

1 The home was inspired by the old farm buildings that dot the Virginia landscape. The asymmetrical window placement adds interest to the unadorned façade, and the generous use of glass keeps the building in close contact with the deck and yard. The three-and-a-half-story plan neatly fits several functions under one roof: a below-grade garage/storage area; a main level entertainment/living room; and a separate upper level guest house.

2 Although it resembles wood, the siding is vertical Hardiboard butted together to create a subtle texture. Unlike wood, Hardiboard requires no maintenance and is impervious to the effects of weather and pests. A tiny window high in the gable serves as both an exterior detail and a way to enhance natural light on the upper level.

rhythmic fenestration kept the house from looking too much like its neighbors while still keeping it in context. "We wanted to capture the romantic qualities of the locale, and above all keep it quiet by using the minimal number of materials and not adding anything that wasn't crucial to the design," Walker says. "The goal was to create the illusion of a silhouette in the landscape, which was made possible by not putting any heavy details on the house. It has a quaint feel to it that really works, and at the same time it functions on numerous levels."

The home's low-maintenance exterior was achieved with vertically butted Hardiboard plank siding, which from a distance resembles wood but is maintenance-free and has the added benefit of being weather- and pest-resistant. "The goal was to bring texture and variation to the building, which is easily done with wood—but wood requires upkeep, and the owner didn't want that," Walker notes. "By using Hardiboard we were able to achieve a fresh look that speaks to the character of the structures in the region and at the same time prevent the house from becoming a lot of work down the road."

Archimania used the window placement as an opportunity to create a visually interesting composition on the exterior.

Rather than a symmetrical placement of glass to match the symmetrical lines of the house, Walker and his colleagues took a cue from their collective portfolio and tweaked the positioning of the windows to add variation to the façade: the lower-level glass doors march obediently along the deck but above they spread out at the living room and squeeze together at the bedroom. "The juxtaposition of the windows really adds something to this elevation," Walker explains. "So now you have a box with a subtle design feature that comes from the windows." In addition, the windows on each end of the building are different shapes and sizes.

The home's three-and-a-half-story floor plan accommodates public and private zones. The first level is designed for pool parties and other events and can be used as a casual living room, and the second floor is a separate guest house complete with kitchen, living/dining room, bedroom and loft. The garage was placed under the building to minimize its presence in the plan. "We wanted to give the upper and lower floors a distinctive feel and atmosphere," Walker explains. "Although the building is small, it can handle a variety of activities at once, which makes it very flexible."

3 The deck overhang, with its exposed rafters connected by a metal pipe, adds a level of detail without being busy or complicated. The canopy protects the glass doors from rain and helps shade the interiors. The deck is ipe, a Brazilian hardwood popular for its durability and beauty.

4 The main-level washroom includes a maple cabinet and a cabinet top and mirror frame made from reclaimed heart pine. The butted vertical wood siding was also reclaimed. The flooring is glass cobblestone tile panels by Ann Sacks.

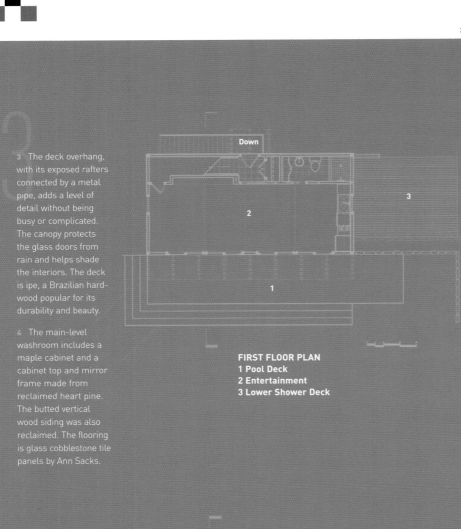

FIRST FLOOR PLAN
1 Pool Deck
2 Entertainment
3 Lower Shower Deck

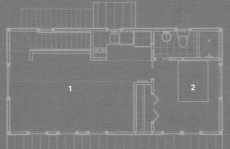

SECOND FLOOR PLAN
1 Gathering
2 Sleeping

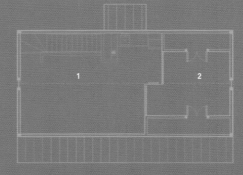

LOFT FLOOR PLAN
1 Open to Below
2 Loft

Up

GARAGE PLAN

5

Large sliding glass doors give the building a strong indoor/outdoor connection. Unlike the top-floor guest house, which has a vaulted ceiling, the lower level has a low ceiling painted in a gold tone to bring warmth to the room. A galley kitchen with painted wood cabinets was placed against the far wall of the room to maximize the square footage.

Guest quarters occupy the entire upper level of the house. The architects designed it to exist independently of the lower level by giving it a kitchen and bedroom and its own entry. The richness of the reclaimed Australian cypress flooring contrasts nicely against the light walls and adds texture to the room. The loft, contained within a steel-and-cable railing, performs double duty as a children's play area and an extra bedroom. A painted wood cabinet topped with a plastic laminate counter provides plenty of storage, which helps keep the small space organized and uncluttered.

Styled like a boutique hotel bathroom, the upper-level lavatory is "a little refuge within the context of the house," the architects explain. Plusher than other areas of the home, it features shimmering glass tile and a custom wood basin cabinet with a glass top; placing a light fixture inside the cabinet turned it into an unusual night-light.

The lower level of the house is suited to casual poolside gatherings.

7

6

8

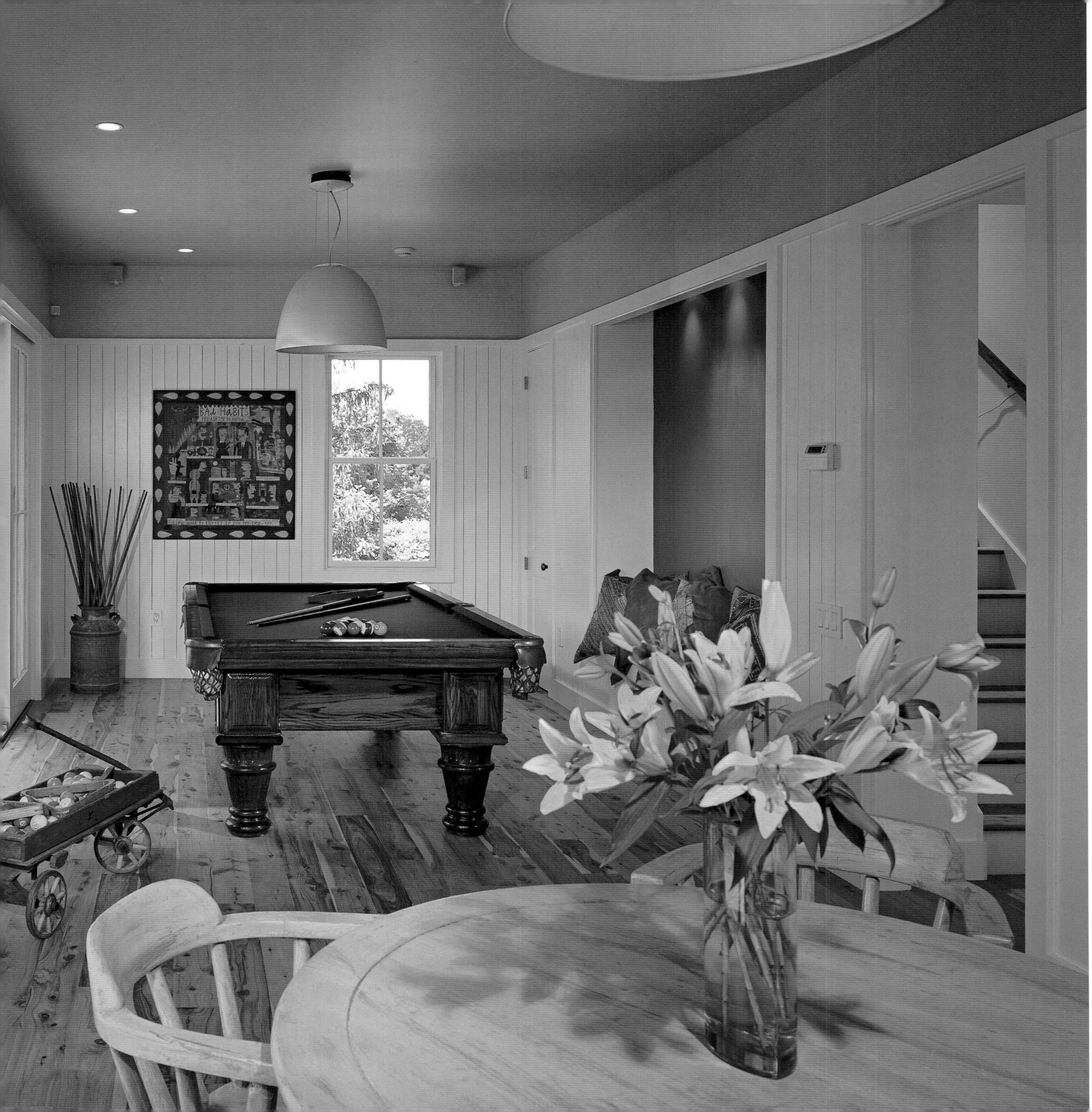

beyond the
traditional cabin

BUILDINGS
THAT FEATURE
CONTEMPORARY
STYLING AND
MATERIALITY
BUT REFLECT A
FAMILIAR CABIN
VERNACULAR

The asymmetrical roof, clad in standing seam zinc, cuts away at the east façade to avoid blocking a window high in the art studio wall. The program specified a transparent house, apparent here in this twilight view. When lit, the vestibule windows are transformed into welcoming lanterns.

european-influenced **alpine dwelling**

DESIGN: RICHARD CIECIUCH, PROJECTWORKSHOP
PHOTOGRAPHS: GERRY EFINGER
LOCATION: TELLURIDE, COLORADO   2,350 SQUARE FEET

This home's meticulous construction and fine materials prompted one person to call it a cabinet in the meadow. The description is fitting: everything about the house, from its evenly spaced wood slat siding to the sleek but warm interior finishes, speaks to high-end craftsmanship and finesse, but this is where the comparison ends. Designer Richard Cieciuch appreciates the romance of the image but is more practical in his thinking: "Aesthetics aside, this is a mountain home that will have to survive the extreme setting," he says. "It has been constructed to withstand whatever the alpine environment might bring—it's very sturdy."

Built for a Munich couple with a passion for art (she owns an art gallery), the 2,350-square-foot "art barn" rests on a patch of pastoral ranch land at 9,700 feet in the San Juan Mountains, near the town of Telluride. The setting is straight out of The Sound of Music—wildflowers dot the meadow in late spring and summer and robust stands of aspen trees provide a kaleidoscopic color show: shifting shades of green during the warmer months, gold and blaze orange in autumn, bare white trunks and branches in winter. As if that weren't enough eye candy, Utah's La Sal Mountains hover on the horizon. Cieciuch says the goal was to balance the more contained foreground views with the panoramic vista. "It was important to prevent the background from becoming overwhelming," he says. "The owners love to see mountains from their windows, but they equally value being in contact with what's happening right around them."

SPECIAL FEATURES FOR THIS PLAN

- FINELY CRAFTED BUT DESIGNED AND BUILT TO WITHSTAND HARSH WINTERS HIGH IN THE COLORADO MOUNTAINS
- CONFIGURED AS TWO DISCRETE SECTIONS—LIVING SPACE AND ART STUDIO—CONNECTED BY A BREEZEWAY THAT ALSO FUNCTIONS AS AN OUTDOOR ROOM
- RIVER-STONE GABION IN LIEU OF A TYPICAL STONE WALL TO BRING COLOR AND TEXTURE TO THE HOUSE WITHOUT WEIGHING IT DOWN

1 A gabion along the base of the east façade is a refined alternative to more rustic and conventional forms of stonework. The designer created a mesh metal bin and filled it with smooth, colorful stones from the Colorado River. The gabion was less time-consuming and thus less expensive than a traditional stone veneer wall. The windows and doors throughout the house are African mahogany.

2 The cabin's design maximizes distant views of Utah's La Sal Mountains and keeps the owners in intimate connection with the sur-

rounding meadows and aspen groves. The low-slung building is appropriately scaled and its careful placement along the contours of the site minimized the cost and effects of excavation.

3 Long-lasting and low-maintenance massaranduba siding brings texture and rich color to the exterior. The boards are backed with insect screen for an elegant black reveal, and exposed glulam rafters establish an eye-catching rhythm that extends from the interiors. Slats at the corner steam shower provide privacy without obstructing the views from inside.

4 The art studio's eighteen-foot-high window is inset with operable hoppers at the top and bottom to enhance fresh air circulation through the space. The wall paneling here and throughout the cabin is rift-cut white oak plywood with a natural finish.

5 Commercial-grade aluminum garage doors can be easily lifted to expose the art studio to the outdoors. The floors are polished concrete with radiant in-floor heat.

Cieciuch, working with carpenter-turned-architect Dylan Henderson, took his initial cues from the regional barn vernacular but updated his building with modern materials and functional living and work spaces. He also studied European mountain houses, in the process developing an appreciation for their "human" scale, appropriately sized floor plans and low-key elegance, he explains. This approach pleased the owners, who weren't keen on a log cabin reenacted in the traditional American style.

The house is divided into two sections: one combines living, dining and sleeping quarters while the other is a spacious, light-filled art studio with a soaring eighteen-foot ceiling and commercial garage doors (in lieu of French or sliding doors) that can be pulled up to fully open the room to the deck, thus expanding its usable dimensions. A breezeway connects the sections and serves another purpose: in cooperative weather it doubles as a covered outdoor room/entertainment patio.

Cieciuch used only a handful of materials on the house, opting for an uncomplicated palette that allows the individual elements to stand out. Massaranduba wood slats clad the exterior and the deck, mahogany plywood covers the breezeway ceiling, and the roofing is beautiful and long-lasting

matte-finish zinc. Rather than follow the crowd and use chunky stone to protect the lower portion of the building from prolonged contact with accumulated snow, Cieciuch chose a veneer that recalls a gabion, a steel mesh structure filled with loose-laid rock, in this case smooth-to-the-touch stones from the Colorado River. The gabion, which runs along the east façade, was less expensive than a regular stone veneer wall and took less time to install. "There's a lot of Colorado geology sitting in that wall," he quips.

Other materials include African mahogany (windows), rift-cut white oak plywood (interior ceiling and walls), mesh steel (railings), solid white oak (counters), glass tile (shower) and polished concrete floors with radiant heat.

To Cieciuch it all comes down to a bigger-picture idea. "Here in the West, the familiar log cabin has shaped many a notion of retreat," he says. "Our goal, which was enthusiastically endorsed by the clients, was to redefine that notion by combining a practical floor plan, sensible form and scale, and simple materials with an extraordinary site to create a lasting and soulful building."

6 The west façade opens up to the setting with ample sliding glass doors and commercial garage doors that encourage indoor/outdoor living. The building was designed for maximum energy efficiency: triple-gasket seals at the doors and windows prevent heat loss, and the use of structural insulated panels resulted in R-values well in excess of local code requirements. Seven-foot roof overhangs protect the deck and help shade the interiors.

7 One of two in the house, the wood-burning fireplace is covered in white oak panels set slightly apart for an interesting geometric effect. The sliding door and glass panel at the vestibule are set on high-end stainless steel track hardware.

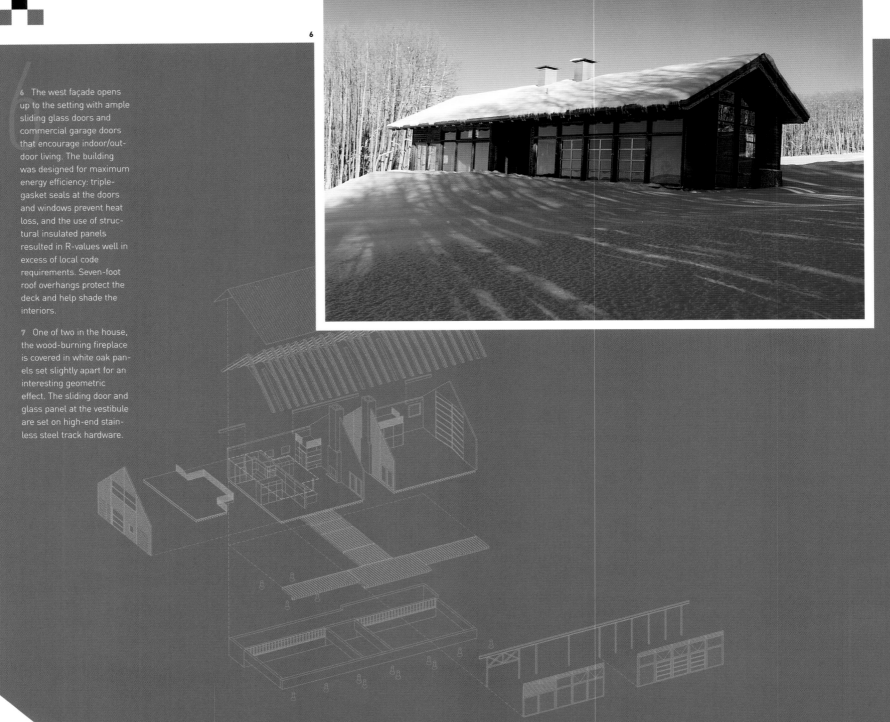

6

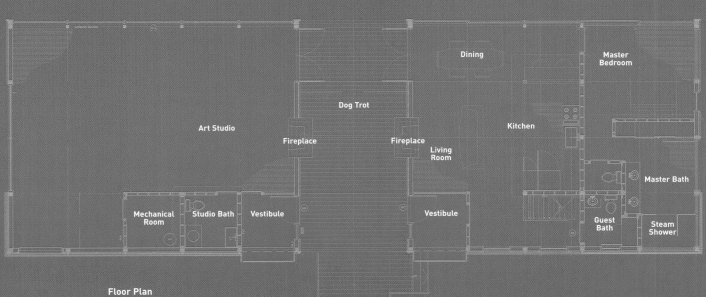

Floor Plan

Art Studio

Dog Trot

Dining

Master Bedroom

Fireplace

Fireplace

Kitchen

Living Room

Mechanical Room

Studio Bath

Vestibule

Vestibule

Master Bath

Guest Bath

Steam Shower

Wood Deck

8 The ceiling, clad in rift-cut white oak plywood panels, is a backdrop for a series of intricately "laced" trusses, which were prefabricated off-site to save time and money. The beams are glulam and the tie rods and connectors are steel. The railing incorporates woven stainless steel mesh skillfully integrated with blackened steel posts by metal artisan Jeff Skoloda.

9 The compact and efficient kitchen is equipped with stainless steel appliances and custom cabinets crafted from white oak. Strategically placed light fixtures on the ceiling showcase the dramatic trusses.

10 The master bathroom includes a spacious steam shower enclosed with floor-to-ceiling glass partially shielded on two sides by an exterior wood slat screen. Pale green glass tiles in the shower bring soft color to the otherwise monochromatic decor. The cabinet and paneling are white oak.

11 The vestibules are a transition between the indoors and outdoors and, thanks to their sturdy and easily cleaned concrete floors, they can handle everything from snow-packed boots to muddy paws. The massaranduba deck is durable enough for long-term mountain use.

2

a view to **san francisco**

DESIGN: FRED HERRING, HERRING AND WORLEY ARCHITECTS

PHOTOGRAPHS: BERNARD ANDRÉ

LOCATION: WOODSIDE, CALIFORNIA   3,000 SQUARE FEET

Tucked away on a heavily treed piece of land and yet close to the amenities of a world-class city—this Northern California home does seem to have it all. The house was designed by Fred Herring for architectural photographer Bernard André, who also asked architect Sanjeev Malhotra to provide input into the floor plan. In the end, all project participants found themselves working toward the common goal of creating a piece of practical, livable art.

The home perches on a sloping 4.8-acre lot in the rolling hills that separate the Bay Area from the Pacific Ocean. Says Herring, "It's conveniently located in terms of its city access, but it seems very far away—you certainly don't feel as if you are in an urban environment."

Despite the generous acreage, Herring faced a number of land-use restrictions and setbacks that meant the house had to be configured to sit on only a small portion of the land. The result is a building that conforms to the mandated building envelope and takes advantage of the one-of-a-kind views and the protection of the surrounding forest. "The site always dictates the design, but in this case it was even more challenging and crucial to find the right balance," Herring notes. "The aim was to work with the requirements of the land and be sure to capture those amazing views of San Francisco and the water."

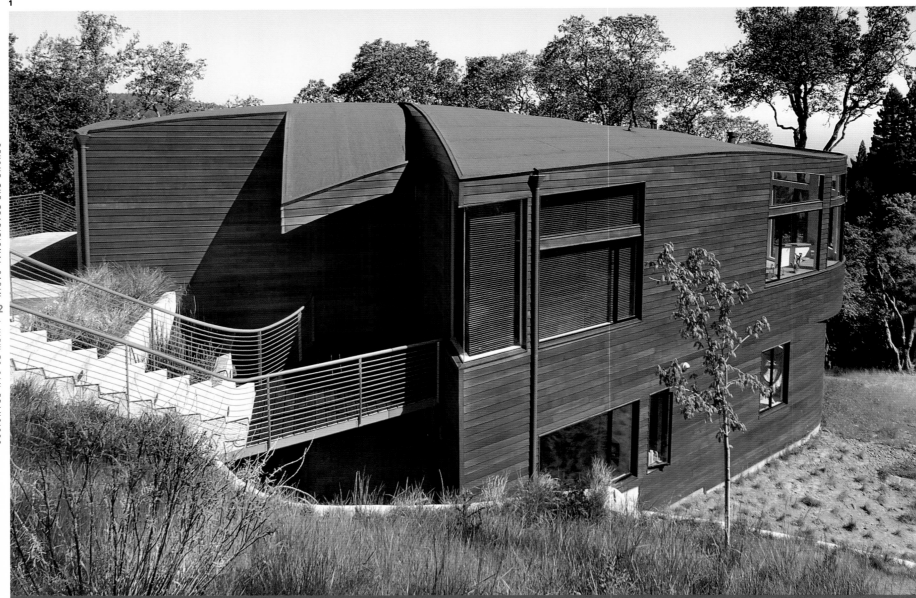

1

SPECIAL FEATURES FOR THIS PLAN

- LUSH, THICKLY FORESTED AND PRIVATE SETTING ONLY MINUTES FROM DOWNTOWN SAN FRANCISCO

- DESIGN THAT COMBINES CURVES AND ANGLES TO FORM A HOME WITH A POLISHED, FINELY CONSTRUCTED APPEARANCE

1 The front entry is protected by a large overhang, and inconspicuous black roll roofing was chosen to allow the house itself to take center stage.

2 The glazed dining room cantilevers ten feet beyond the building, extending into the forest like a tree house platform.

3 The slate-clad dining patio off the kitchen is sheltered from the prevailing winds, making it a comfortable outdoor room even on breezy days. The gentle curve in the roof helps divert rainwater away from the patio, and the railing is wrought iron.

The exterior of the home reveals a rhythmical integration of form and material. Smooth, curved walls, exact corners and into-the-trees projections combine to create a structure that looks as crafted and fitted as a piece of fine furniture. The limited building envelope, Herring explains, called for a concentrated, efficient floor plan; in this case, the main rooms radiate off a central stair that wends its way through three levels. "It's a traditional plan in the organizational sense," the architect says. "But the dramatic shapes of its various elements prevent it from looking traditional."

The home's practical nature is expressed through its down-to-earth materials, which include stained cedar siding, slate patio pavers, wrought-iron railings and black roll roofing. Inside, the soft neutral colors used on the walls and floors become a backdrop for the trees, which in some areas nearly brush up against the windows. To meet their budget, the owners bartered photography services for materials and labor—a great way to save money. And they were willing to purchase off-the-shelf cabinets and other items and then customize them with their own special touches and finishes—another way to trim dollars from a budget without sacrificing quality or aesthetics.

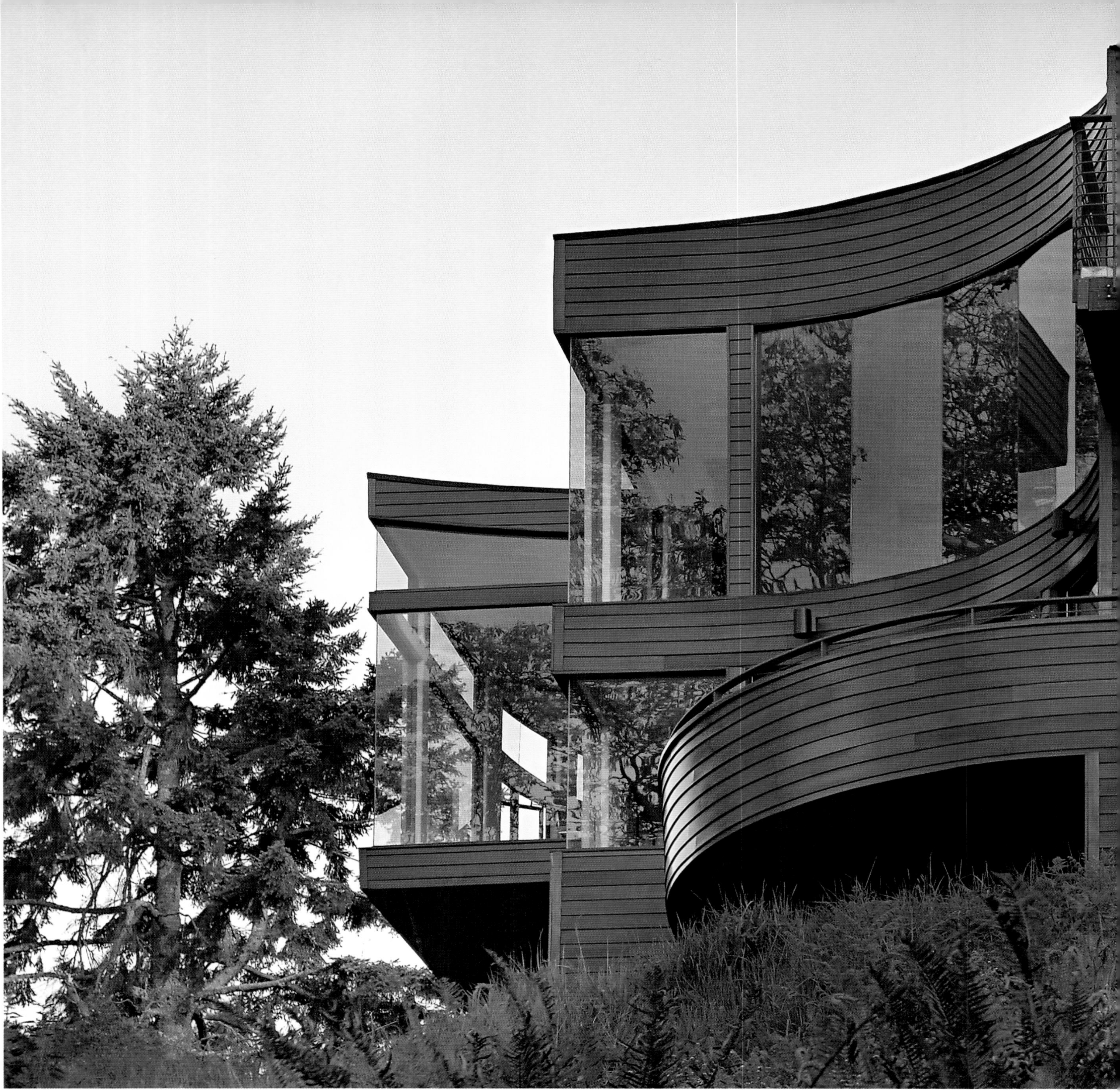

4 Cedar siding finished with a light stain to prevent graying imparts a refined, elegant look to the exterior and places the spotlight on the precise connections between the building's sensuous curves and sharp angles. Ample deck space and glazing promote an indoor/outdoor connection.

5 The reading nook at the far end of the living room has space-saving built-in bench seating.

6 The kitchen faces east to capture soft morning light. The owners purchased off-the-shelf cabinets and then customized them with limestone countertops.

7 The minimalist living room is finished in crisp, light tones, and floor-to-ceiling windows bring nature up close and personal. The flooring is a durable acrylic resin with a concrete base.

6

The aim was to work with the requirements of the land and be sure to capture those amazing views of San Francisco and the water.

slopeside mining **vernacular**

DESIGN: DAVID WEBBER, WEBBER HANZLIK ARCHITECTS
PHOTOGRAPHS: KEN GUTMAKER
LOCATION: ANGEL FIRE, NEW MEXICO   2,300 SQUARE FEET

Architect David Webber found his inspiration in history when hired to design this northern New Mexico retreat. Evident are the steep angles and industrial materiality of the area's old mining structures but in this case they have been used to compose an up-to-date version of the getaway house that puts function and practicality at the top of the priorities list.

The 2,300-square-foot cabin is located at a breath-sapping 10,000 feet on a ski-in/ski-out site in the Angel Fire ski resort near Taos. Configured to comfortably sleep twelve, the house "breaks with local traditions while still recalling them," Webber says. This was especially important to one of the owners, who spent her childhood summers at a bare-bones cabin in the northeastern part of the state. "By reintroducing the dramatic forms typical of mountain-style, heavy timber construction and the social aspects of lodge architecture in an abstracted way, we were able to instill new life into the regional aesthetic," Webber explains.

The house appears as a set of variously proportioned slopes placed closely together, but the effect is anything but hodgepodge. Rather, the exterior elements come together through material and color to exhibit an eye-pleasing sense of scale. "Placing a low-pitched roof next to a tall roof, for example, gave the building a lot of expression,"

SPECIAL FEATURES FOR THIS PLAN

- CONTEMPORARY MOUNTAIN LODGE HOUSE THAT COMBINES ELEMENTS OF HISTORICAL MINING AND LODGE ARCHITECTURE

- OPEN FLOOR PLAN WITH TUCKED-AWAY PLACES FOR RELAXATION AND SLEEPING

1 The southwest-facing façade settles into the site and reveals a palette of exterior materials firmly rooted in regional influence, including corrugated metal (siding and roof), stucco (dark gray areas), fir (window trim) and steel (railings). The roof overhangs terminate at a sharp point for an elegant, refined edge.

2 Materials were chosen for aesthetics and long-term durability—the latter attribute particularly important for a rugged, mountainous site.

other accents, and applied metal panels in shades of gray and pale yellow to the gables to bring texture and color to the house.

This theme of refined rusticity continues inside. The great room–style floor plan is appropriately casual, and an inglenook adjacent to the main living area is a magnet for those seeking solitude (it also doubles as sleeping quarters). Interior materials include pine floors, cedar window trim, vertical-grain Douglas fir cabinetry and galvanized metal counters. A wall of glass in the great room sends sunlight into the rooms and focuses on nearby Wheeler Peak. Two large closets are equipped with built-in bunks, and the master bedroom overlooks the great room below through swinging barn doors.

"The goal was to include public and private spaces throughout the house," Webber says. "This way, people can stay connected if they want or they can move away from the activity in the house to enjoy some quiet time."

Webber explains. "This house is a marriage between mining and lodge architecture, from its overall presentation to the selection of materials inside and out."

Part of the cabin's appeal is its solidity. Webber, cognizant of issues of long-term maintenance and durability, was diligent about designing a house that could withstand the sometimes-harsh realities of life in thin air. Working with a restricted budget, he chose maintenance-free corrugated metal for the roof and portions of the siding, poured-in-place concrete for the patios and decks, steel for the railings and

3

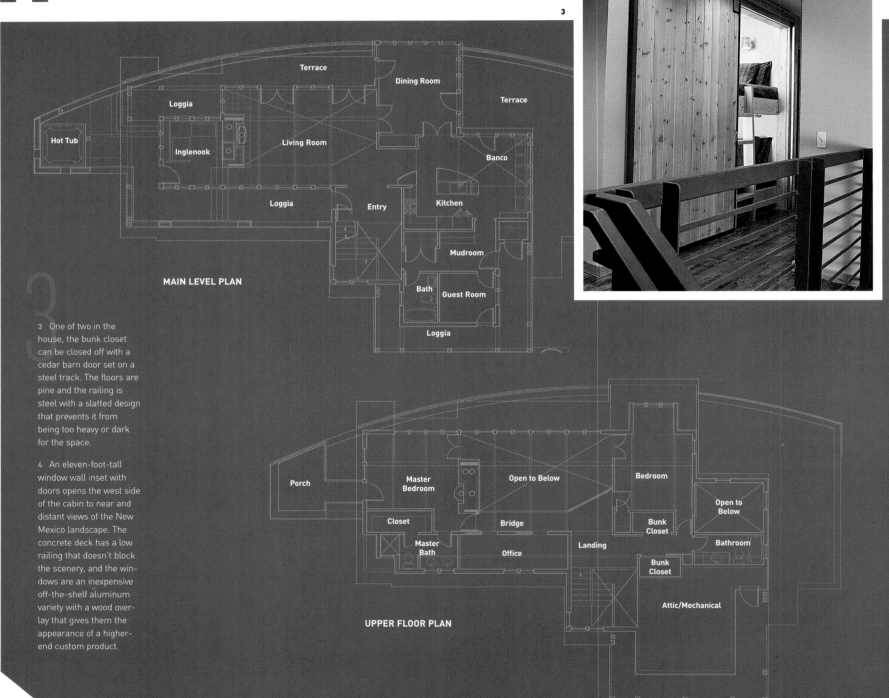

Terrace

Dining Room

Loggia

Terrace

Hot Tub

Living Room

Inglenook

Banco

Loggia

Entry

Kitchen

MAIN LEVEL PLAN

Mudroom

Bath

Guest Room

Loggia

3 One of two in the house, the bunk closet can be closed off with a cedar barn door set on a steel track. The floors are pine and the railing is steel with a slatted design that prevents it from being too heavy or dark for the space.

4 An eleven-foot-tall window wall inset with doors opens the west side of the cabin to near and distant views of the New Mexico landscape. The concrete deck has a low railing that doesn't block the scenery, and the windows are an inexpensive off-the-shelf aluminum variety with a wood overlay that gives them the appearance of a higher-end custom product.

Porch

Master Bedroom

Open to Below

Bedroom

Closet

Bridge

Open to Below

Bunk Closet

Master Bath

Office

Landing

Bathroom

Bunk Closet

Attic/Mechanical

UPPER FLOOR PLAN

4

93

BEYOND THE TRADITIONAL CABIN   SLOPESIDE MINING VERNACULAR

5 The owners are avid cooks but preferred a pared-down kitchen over one filled with all the latest gadgets. Galvanized metal counters and cabinet fronts are durable and require little maintenance, and the open-shelf portions of the upper cabinets can be hidden behind metal panels that slide across the openings on basic track hardware. The cabinets reveal the beauty of locally harvested fir.

6 With its twenty-foot-high exposed-truss ceiling, cedar-trimmed windows and sculptural steel wood-burning fireplace set into a stucco alcove, the great room has the atmosphere of a classic lodge.

7 One of two in the house, the bunk closet can be closed off with a cedar barn door set on a steel track. The floors are pine and the railing is steel with a slatted design that prevents it from being too heavy or dark for the space.

8 An exposed truss in the master bedroom helps scale the room for maximum comfort and livability. The paint colors are meant to evoke the fresh green of new aspen leaves and the creamy gray-white of the trees' trunks. Swinging barn doors connect the space to the great room below.

9 An inglenook adjacent to the great room features vertical-grain fir and built-in benches that are deep enough to be used as beds.

9

A two-story window wall on the south elevation connects the upper and lower floors and fills the stairwell with natural light. Although it looks custom (and, thus, expensive), the wall was made with standard windows in a variety of sizes. The windows are clad in aluminum outside and hemlock inside, and sections of the glazing are operable for cross ventilation.

high design, **low budget**

DESIGN: ERIC LOGAN

PHOTOGRAPHS: PAUL WARCHOL

LOCATION: TETON VALLEY, WYOMING   2,400 SQUARE FEET

From a design and livability perspective this stylish, light-filled getaway is miles away from the log cabin the owners occupied for years. After too many cold winters and days filled in dark, uninviting rooms, they decided it was time for a radical change. They sold the cabin, which ended up being moved to another site for use by a new owner, and hired architect Eric Logan to create their dream home based on the following parameters: make it small but comfortable, casual and, above all, affordable.

Logan didn't shy away from his clients' tight budget and request for a simple floor plan with a bit of flair. In the end he accomplished both goals for a reasonable $160 per square foot, a price that when compared to the residential market in and around high-end Jackson is a bargain. His trick? Connected, flowing spaces (open plans are less costly than those with lots of walls and hallways) and off-the-shelf materials such as medium-density fiberboard (MDF), Masonite, concrete and steel used in a manner that brought sophistication to the house without breaking the budget. "These materials really speak for themselves," Logan says. "They have their own inherent beauty and as a bonus

SPECIAL FEATURES FOR THIS PLAN

- EVERYDAY MATERIALS THAT APPEAR MORE EXPENSIVE THAN THE BUDGET WOULD INDICATE

- DRAMATIC TWO-STORY WINDOW WALL THAT HAS A CUSTOM APPEARANCE BUT WAS ASSEMBLED WITH OFF-THE-SHELF PRODUCTS

they happen to be economical. This is a good example of high design on a low budget."

The two-story house sits nestled at the base of a hill. Logan wisely incorporated the contours of the site into the design, positioning the house to work with the land rather than against it—another money-saving move. The first floor anchors the building into the hill while the second floor, which contains the primary living functions, rises into the tree canopy. Thick stands of privacy-enhancing trees on the south and east sides of the house allowed for the installation of broad expanses of glass, crucial to the airy, buoyant atmosphere the owners craved. "The second floor has the feel of a tree house," Logan says. "You have these beautifully filtered mountain views and wonderful year-round light, and there's a real intimacy with the setting."

The budget etched in his mind, Logan decided that the most cost-effective program for the house would be the most straightforward. He drew a basic box embellished with what he describes as "articulations" meant to add variation and interest to the façade. "The idea was to make the box more than a box by carving away corners and pulling parts of the house out into projections that extend from the living areas," he explains. "This technique

effectively breaks up the mass of the structure; without them it would not have the texture and shadow-play now evident on each elevation."

Logan also used standard prefabricated trusses and floor joists to save money and chose affordable and long-lasting oxidized steel siding. Other budget-conscious material selections included MDF (interior built-ins) and Masonite (indoor wall and window trim) and the spare use of cedar siding to cut costs and bring warmth to the steel box. One of the home's most striking features is a two-story glass wall at the stairwell that might appear to be expensive but was, in fact, budget-friendly: Logan clipped together standard windows in varying sizes, and the result is a window that cleverly belies its price tag.

Logan is grateful to his clients for giving him the freedom to seek out new ways to express the elegance of basic forms and common materials. "They didn't have a lot of preconceived notions about the design, so there was a lot of room for exploration," he says, voicing what must be every architect's dream. In return, this couple now has a retreat that works in every aspect for their lifestyle—as well as money left over to spend on other pursuits.

1 The owners' limited budget dictated a simple, straightforward design, but the architect was able to animate the façade with projections that extend from the main living areas. A steel visor placed over the band of clerestory windows brings texture to the façade—and at minimal expense. Economical oxidized steel panels

refer to the region's agricultural history and complement the cedar siding.

2 The architect increased the distance between the cedar siding boards at the base of the house, a no-cost way to add visual variation to the exterior.

3 The small study adjacent to the master bedroom has a narrow window positioned high on the wall to provide a close-up view of the site's abundant aspen trees. Pale green paint imparts a soothing ambience to the room.

4 The living room features a built-in shelving/media center crafted from MDF and equipped with a panel that slides on barn track hardware to hide the television and stereo. The vertical window to the right is trimmed in Masonite and positioned to frame a glimpse of an aspen grove.

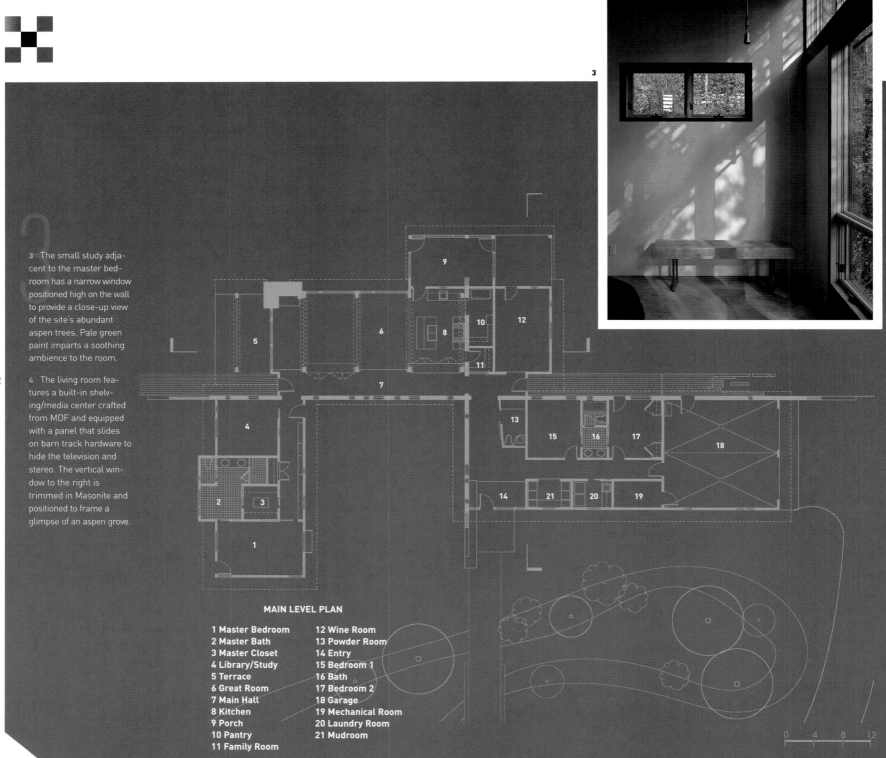

3

MAIN LEVEL PLAN

1 Master Bedroom	12 Wine Room
2 Master Bath	13 Powder Room
3 Master Closet	14 Entry
4 Library/Study	15 Bedroom 1
5 Terrace	16 Bath
6 Great Room	17 Bedroom 2
7 Main Hall	18 Garage
8 Kitchen	19 Mechanical Room
9 Porch	20 Laundry Room
10 Pantry	21 Mudroom
11 Family Room	

0   4   8   12

5 The architect used horizontal cedar boards inside and out to bring continuity to the design and keep the materials palette as pared-down as possible, which in turn saved money. A continuous clerestory window in the main hall sends light into the space, and the steel visor over the window throws a pattern of light onto the floor.

6 The architect used Masonite for portions of the interior trim. A recycled sheet product readily available at home-improvement stores, Masonite is inexpensive and, when finished with linseed oil as shown here, deepens to a rich gray-brown sheen. The private setting allowed for the generous use of glass.

7

8

7 The reading area, an intimate nook within the great room, is located in the projected box. The space is clad in low-cost MDF panels with a clear-coat finish and trimmed in hemlock. Operable hoppers at the base of the window ensure ventilation and concrete floors absorb warmth from the sun, adding to the comfort of the room and helping to reduce energy bills.

8 The steel visor partially encloses and shades the deck and its slatted design sends a play of light and shadow through the interiors.

The architects allowed the contours of the meadow to direct the design, and the result is a building that seems to grow out of the gently sloping hillside.

texas hill country **getaway**

DESIGN: ELIZABETH DANZE AND JOHN BLOOD, DANZE AND BLOOD ARCHITECTS

PHOTOGRAPHS: GREG HURSLEY

LOCATION: MARBLE FALLS, TEXAS   2,600 SQUARE FEET

The setting is idyllic: a stand of live oaks and madrone trees amid a wildflower meadow on a three-hundred-acre working ranch in the famed Texas Hill Country. Designed for a couple who wanted a family-friendly retreat from urban life in nearby Austin as well as a place suitable for corporate events, the house meets both needs with understated elegance and a sense of rugged sturdiness, Texas-style.

The combined vision of architects Elizabeth Danze and John Blood, the 2,600-square-foot house hunkers down into its site, creating the effect, says Blood, "of a house that appears to be rising up from the meadow. The site just called for a house that grew out of the land."

The building's angularity and simple palette speak to a modern ethic but the materials, primarily cedar, ponderosa pine and limestone, keep the home rooted to its Texas origins. "There is a real earthiness to the house, and we were careful to relate it to the land," says Danze. "What you see is clean and in some ways spare but at the same time warm and welcoming."

SPECIAL FEATURES FOR THIS PLAN

- ELABORATE TRUSS SYSTEM THAT DEFINES THE INTERIORS AND FORMS A DRAMATIC DISPLAY AT THE ROOFLINE

- SIMILAR MATERIALS USED INSIDE AND OUT FOR CONTINUITY AND TO KEEP THE PALETTE AS STREAMLINED AS POSSIBLE

1 The house sits low to the ground in a stand of live oak and madrone trees and overlooks a three-hundred-acre working ranch. A long roof with exaggerated overhangs protects the house from the elements and also functions as a type of enclosure.

2 The primary exterior materials are stained cedar siding and limestone at the fireplace, shown here. The thick base of the fireplace anchors the house to the ground and tapers as it rises.

3 Deep overhangs shelter the house from sun and rain. The standing seam metal roof will last for years and require little maintenance.

Two defining features—one outside, one inside—work in tandem to characterize the home. The first is a low-slung standing seam metal roof that extends over the decks and pathways to serve as shelter from sun and rain; the roof, however, goes beyond its original duty to become a sort of truncated enclosure over the house. The second is a series of trusses positioned along the length of the building; constructed of sturdy ponderosa pine, the trusses are a visual treat and an effective interior organizing element. Only partially structural, the trusses nonetheless do help support the roof but as Blood points out, "They are more about celebrating structure and creating an unforgettable presence in the house."

Danze and Blood, who are based in Austin, understand the vagaries of the Texas weather and as such designed this house for all seasons. The trick, Danze says, was to instill an easy flow between inside and out, with the result a direct indoor/outdoor orientation of space that keeps the owners in contact with the landscape. In addition to a large screened porch (perfect for being outside without being outside, so to speak), the home has wide French doors at the sitting area that open the interior rooms to the fresh air. Excessive solar gain is mitigated by the large overhangs, and a firepit can turn any night into an evening under the stars.

4 The entry hall features a built-in honed lime-stone display case (to the right) specially designed for the owners' collection of arrowheads and fossils.

5 The successful juxta-position of wood and stone is visible in the great room. This view into the main living area is through a massive cutout in the fireplace. Although the form of the house is simple, the architects used flourishes such as this to create a custom home like no other.

6 The trusses, con-structed of ponderosa pine and positioned to line up with the ridge line of the roof, run the length of the house and provide the basic organization of the building. The archi-tects chose ponderosa for its sturdiness as well as for its rich color, and repeated it in other indoor applications as a comple-ment to the exterior cedar. A stone wall serves as a functional divider within the floor plan, and the angled limestone fire-place adds visual drama. The floors are sealed concrete.

MAIN FLOOR PLAN

1 Firepit
2 Bedroom
3 Bath
4 Closet
5 Dressing
6 Mechanical
7 Entry
8 Living Room
9 Bedroom
10 Kitchen
11 Utility
12 Screened Porch
13 Pool

6

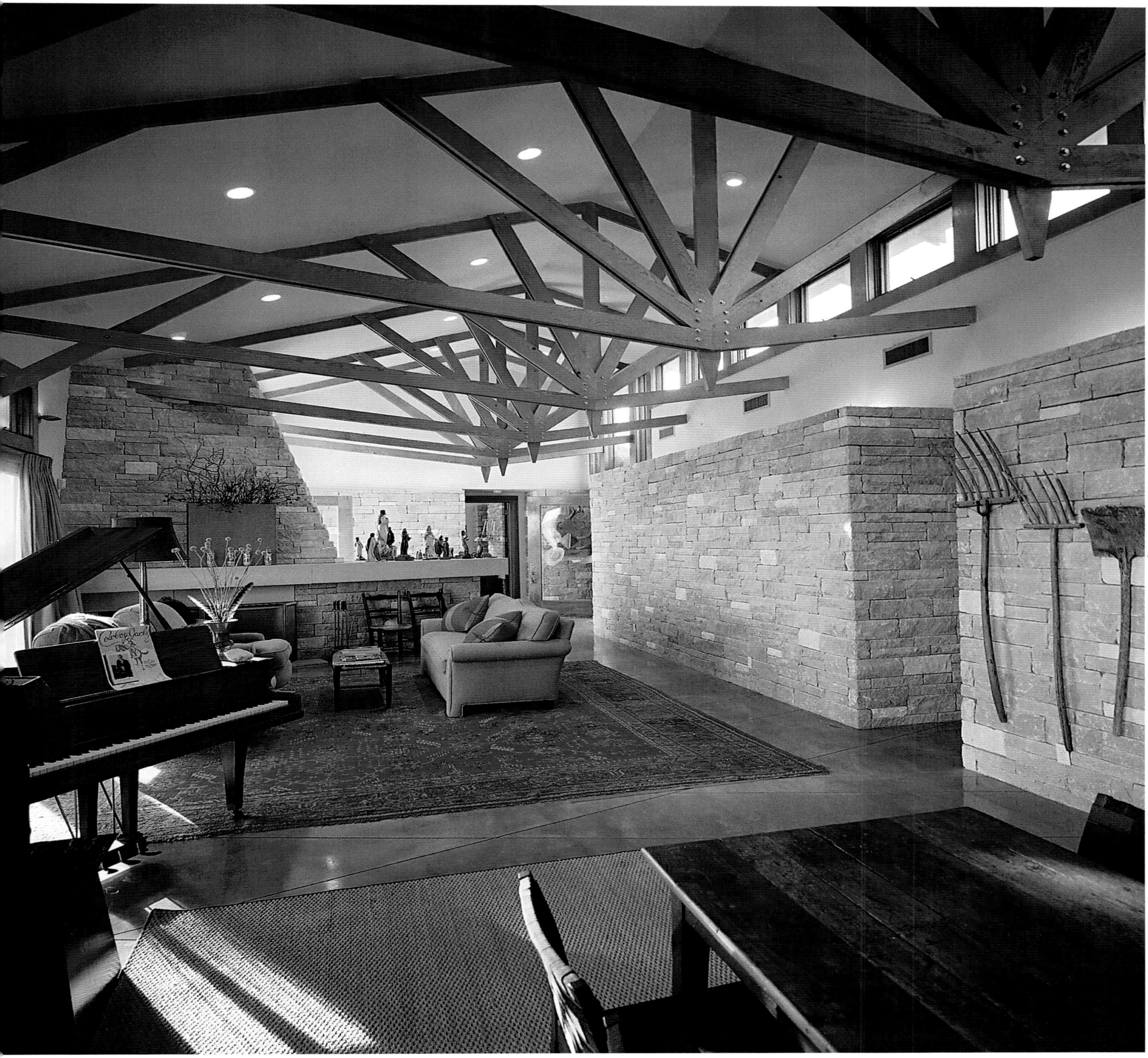

7 A screened porch on one end of the cabin serves as a transitional space between the indoors and outdoors. The roof is composed of two angled planes that run the length of the building.

8 Wide cedar-trimmed French doors connect the sitting room to a porch, and motorized clerestory windows above the doors can be opened for extra ventilation. Although similar materials were used inside and out, the interiors reveal a more refined application of wood and stone.

There is a real earthiness to the house, and we were careful to relate it to the land . . . what you see is clean and in some ways spare but at the same time warm and welcoming.

9 Slate tile and marble counters bring texture and color to the master bath.

10 The cabin's bold lines are continued in the master bedroom. The bed is centered on the stone wall and flanked by limestone nightstands attached to the wall.

02

SECTION

harnessing the sun

DESIGN: KEVIN BURKE, CARNEY ARCHITECTS
PHOTOGRAPHS: CHRISTIE GOSS
LOCATION: JACKSON, WYOMING 4,500 SQUARE FEET

This house near the town of Jackson has a bold contemporary façade but Kevin Burke and his colleagues at Carney Architects made it more than a strong architectural statement by turning it into an energy-efficient mountain retreat that can go without air-conditioning in summer and requires only minimal heating even during the darkest days of winter.

The home is configured to fit the steep site and limited building envelope. Visually, the façade is dominated by a long, sweeping roof and a copper-clad projection on the tallest side. From the beginning of the design process, the owners expressed their desire for alternative energy sources and affordable, durable materials. One of the owners, a scientist, helped Burke research passive-solar options and other ways to lessen the home's impact on the grid. The result is a house that harnesses the powerful rays of the sun for the purposes of heating and some electricity generation and has operable windows in every room for cross ventilation and natural light.

SPECIAL FEATURES FOR THIS PLAN

- PASSIVE SOLAR DESIGN THAT CAPITALIZES ON WYOMING'S ABUNDANT SUNSHINE TO HEAT THE INTERIORS AND DRASTICALLY REDUCE HEATING BILLS

- CLEVER AND AFFORDABLE SHUTTER SYSTEM THAT ALLOWS THE OWNERS TO CLOSE UP THE HOME AT NIGHT TO RETAIN THE PRECIOUS HEAT GAINED DURING THE DAY

2

The siting of the house represented a significant challenge, Burke says, namely how to capture sunlight in winter, when the sun disappears behind the mountain peaks early in the day. "There weren't many solar opportunities to begin with, but we were able to make this work by carefully studying the path of the sun and raising the height of the building on one end to enhance sun exposure," he says.

Solar panels positioned below the main patio conform to the subdivision's design guidelines and are understated to the point that, from a distance, they resemble the copper cladding used on the exterior of the building. The solar issue resolved, the architects went on to complete a house that at the time had the distinction of being the most energy-efficient residence on record in the county. Admirably modest, Burke gives credit to the owner, who devised an ingenious and low-cost solution to preventing the free heat from the sun from draining out through the windows at night: fabric-covered foam panels crafted into insulating shutters. "Even glass with high thermal properties loses heat as sunlight diminishes," Burke explains. "The shutters add

insulation value to the glass and do an amazing job of keeping the indoors warm. During the day you get this wonderful passive solar effect and then at night you can button up the house by closing the shutters against the cold."

For even greater energy efficiency, Burke used structural insulated panels (SIPS) for the roof; SIPS are quick to install and can substantially augment a home's heat-retaining qualities. Other materials include cedar siding, copper cladding inside and out, a standing seam metal roof, alder, and decking made from a combination of recycled plastic and wood.

Did these eco-friendly measures add up to unwelcome budget overruns? According to Burke, no. "We were looking at maybe a few percentage points higher in terms of expense," he says, "but over the long term, the gains will more than pay for that slight increase, and the owners will continue to feel good about doing their part to help the planet."

1 The shape of the house was dictated by the sloping site, limited building envelope and neighborhood height restrictions. A long, sweeping roof became the driving force of the design and allowed for a double-height façade on one end to maximize solar exposure. Windows in every room harness sunlight for passive heating, and solar thermal panels heat water for domestic use and for the home's radiant in-floor heating system. The house has also been set up to receive future photovoltaic panels for electricity generation and storage.

2 The decking is a long-lasting and maintenance-free combination of recycled wood and plastic, and the railing was made from inexpensive recycled steel rods and tubes. The lower windows are operable awnings, which in combination with higher windows draw in cooling breezes to help maintain a comfortable temperature inside the house on hot days.

3

MAIN FLOOR PLAN

1 Office
2 Master Bedroom
3 Master Bath
4 Closet
5 Great Room
6 Kitchen
7 Entry
8 Mudroom/Laundry
9 Garage
10 Covered Deck
11 Deck

SITE ELEVATION

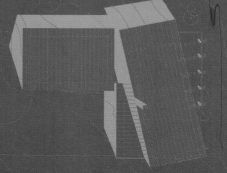

4

3   The main patio, located just off the kitchen, is oriented to the south and east.

4   Vertical cedar siding emphasizes the horizontality of the roof, constructed of structural insulated panels (SIPS). SIPS are cost-effective, can be installed quickly, and have impressive thermal values.

FIRST FLOOR PLAN

UPPER FLOOR PLAN

1 Shop
2 Crawlspace
3 Guest Room
4 Guest Room
5 Mechanical
6 Patio

1 Guest Room
2 Bath
3 Closet
4 Open to Below

5 The living room reveals the down-to-earth nature of the interiors. A transparent steel railing similar to those outside the house prevents the space from becoming too visually divided.

6 Alder cabinets and solid-surface countertops worked with the owners' budget. Although the counters resemble granite, they were much less expensive and did not compromise the quality of the interior finishes.

7 Insulating shutters, crafted by the owners out of fabric-covered foam panels, can be closed at night to prevent the loss of heat accumulated during the day. The shutters greatly enhance the thermal value of the window glass, which has resulted in reduced heating costs.

6

7

The shape of the house—
two boxes joined by a
breezeway—was driven
by budget and a simple,
modular design. Ample
glass on the south
façade ensures that the
interiors receive plenty of
natural light.

simple, functional, **highly livable**

DESIGN: JOHN KLOPF, KLOPF ARCHITECTURE

PHOTOGRAPHS: KEN GUTMAKER

LOCATION: FAIRFIELD, CALIFORNIA   1,350 SQUARE FEET

Compromise is paramount in marriage—perhaps as important as hiring the right architect. This contemporary California retreat meets the needs of a design-savvy couple with a floor plan that addresses the common desire in relationships for connection and separation.

The 1,350-square-foot structure takes practicality and budget considerations to an aesthetic level while keeping the program as pared-down as possible, explains architect John Klopf. The house—two boxes joined by a breeze-way—has zones of privacy tucked into an easygoing floor plan. One of the owners gets up early in the morning to work in her home office, Klopf notes, while the other prefers to stay up late at night and sleep in. Neither of them liked the idea of sectioning off the house with doors and hallways (which would have increased costs), but the solution turned out to be both elegant and budget-conscious: use the breezeway to link the main living area with a self-contained master bedroom suite.

Klopf arranged the rooms in a straight line and repeated certain details—for example, the ceiling structure and the windows—through each space. "The plan facilitates openness and communication, which gives the owners an

1, 2

SPECIAL FEATURES FOR THIS PLAN

- FLOOR PLAN THAT PROVIDES "ALONE TIME" ZONES WHILE ENSURING THAT THE LINES OF COMMUNICATION REMAIN OPEN BETWEEN THOSE IN THE HOUSE
- LIGHT SHELF THAT CONTROLS THE INTENSITY OF SUNLIGHT INSIDE THE HOUSE, KEEPING IT COMFORTABLE EVEN ON THE HOTTEST DAYS OF THE SUMMER

3

1 Crisp detailing and basic forms kept the budget in check but special features, such as the light-controlling awnings, prevent the house from appearing plain. The siding is Forest Stewardship Council (FSC)–certified redwood, a sustainable material with a rich texture and tone.

2 The house is nestled in a mixed forest of manzanita, bamboo and oak trees and sits on a concrete slab, which acts as a physical and visual transition between the controlled environment (the house) and the natural setting. Operable windows release heat as it rises toward the ceiling—

especially welcome on triple-digit summer days.

3 Operable clerestory windows effectively ventilate the interiors, and oversized awnings help control and direct sunlight.

awareness of each other in the house," he says. "And, this alignment of simple details and dividing lines from space to space creates a living environment that is very composed and quiet. I like to think the house shows the warmer side of modern architecture."

Air-conditioning is the norm in this locale but Klopf's clients wanted a more environmentally friendly solution to staying cool. The architect's plan performs a bit of magic: it welcomes sunlight but in a highly controlled manner. Klopf tested a model of the house on a heliodon, a device that simulates the arc of the sun across the sky and indicates where rays will hit a building at various times during the day. Although the south façade of this house is mostly glass, Klopf engineered the design to prevent the interiors from overheating while keeping the quality of light even and consistent, with no "hot spots" or areas of glare. Large exterior overhangs and an indoor light shelf attached to the length of the main wall provide shade and redirect light onto the ceiling. In addition, operable clerestory windows

work in tandem with the lower windows to allow hot air to rise up and out of the building. In winter, lower-angle sunlight hits the concrete floors, warming them and in turn helping to lower heating costs.

Sustainability and a natural look were important to the owners, and Klopf responded by siding the house in Forest Stewardship Council (FSC)–certified redwood siding. Other materials include a standing seam metal roof, stained concrete floors and natural slate tile.

4 The master suite is connected to the main living area with a breeze-way; this arrangement of space worked well for the owners, who keep different sleep schedules.

4

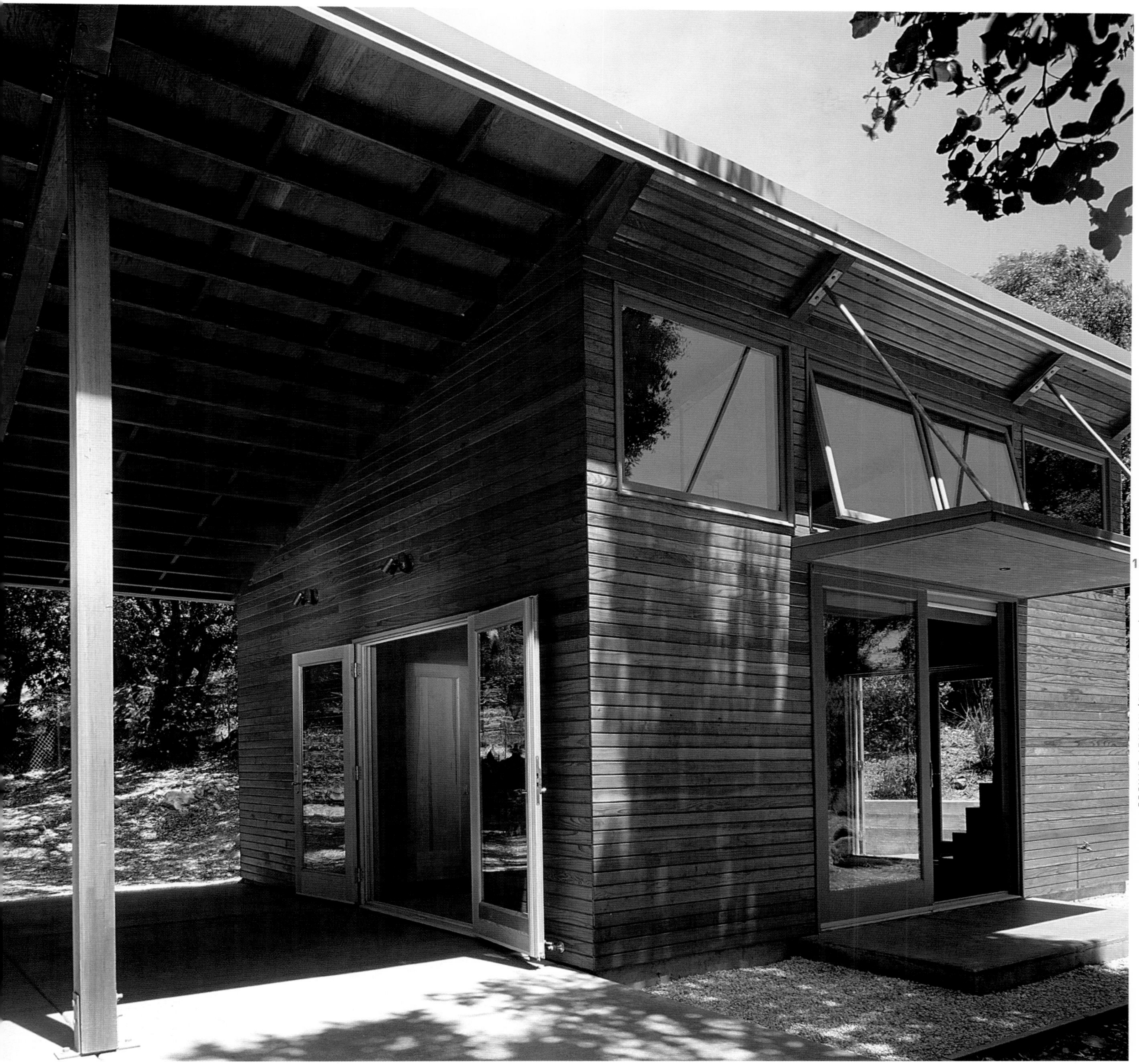

5   The home's stream-lined façade reveals that simplicity can become an aesthetic statement.

6   The architect employed a clever trick to save his clients money: he topped the kitchen island with a slab of granite but used less-expensive matching granite tile on the rest of the counters. The kitchen showcases the beauty of maple plywood.

7   The separate master suite has glass on three sides and a band of clerestory windows; the owners say they feel as though they're camping out thanks to this intimate interaction with the site.

8   The main attraction in the master suite is a Japanese soaking tub crafted from Alaskan yellow cedar. Slate tile adds varie-gated color to the room.

7

133

8

This alignment of simple details and dividing lines from space to space create a living environment that is very composed. I like to think the house shows the warmer side of modern architecture.

9 The larger of the two boxes combines the living, kitchen and dining areas and an office/guest room in one open space kept free of walls and hallways—a tried-and-true money-saving technique. The exposed ceiling beams reflect the structure of the house and leaving them uncovered also saved money. Concrete floors are easy to clean and throw off heat when warmed by the sun, and light-colored maple veneer cabinetry brings a clean, uncluttered look to the space.

10 Operable clerestory windows above the light shelf ventilate the room and keep it comfortable even on the hottest days of the year. The gray panel behind the fireplace is inset with sliding doors on each side that can be pulled out to close off the room.

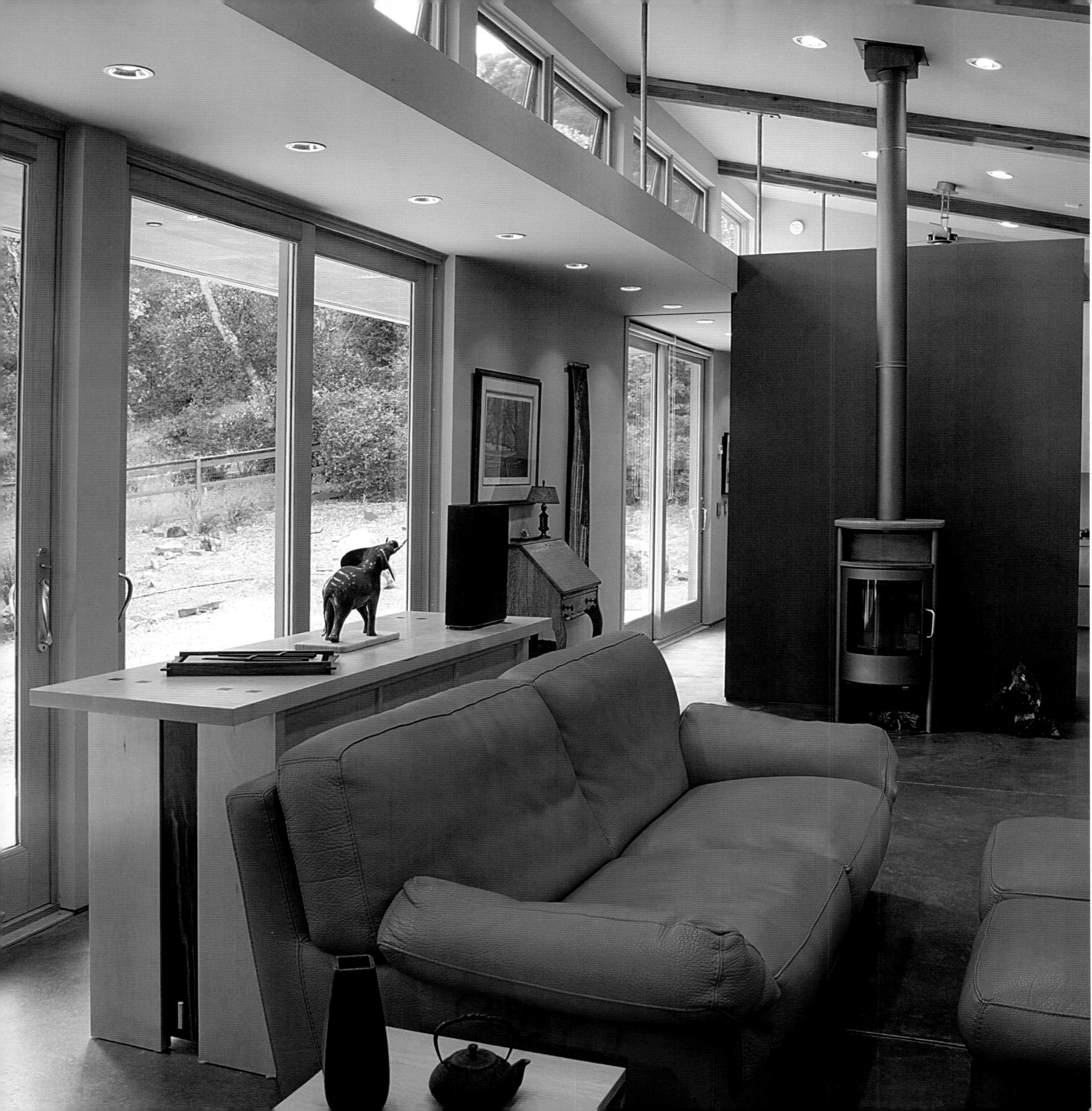

into

the future

**MODERN IN
EVERY WAY: NEW
IDEAS FOR
BUILDING AND
OUTFITTING A
CABIN RETREAT**

private sleeping **cabin**

DESIGN: MICHAEL TAYLOR, TAYLOR SMYTH ARCHITECTS
PHOTOGRAPHS: BEN RAHN, A-FRAME
LOCATION: LAKE SIMCOE, ONTARIO   275 SQUARE FEET

For this Toronto couple, getting away from it all raised an important issue: their lakeside retreat outside the city had become a favorite destination not just for them, but also for friends and family. Although the couple was pleased that their weekend home could comfortably accommodate large gatherings, over time they began to desire a little place of their own.

The couple hired Michael Taylor to design a separate sleeping cabin that would remain visually connected to the main cottage but sit far enough away for complete privacy. "Because of the way the cabin is sited, we were able to turn it into what is essentially a glass box covered on two sides with a cedar slat screen for privacy where needed," he explains.

The screen also gives the 275-square-foot cabin its unique appearance. Taylor arranged the slats to form a delicate pattern, increasing the gaps between the wood pieces arbitrarily on the side of the building nearest the lake. The effect is dramatic: sunlight hitting the cabin creates a shimmering effect, an architectural optical illusion achieved with minimal expense. "As the sun sets, the varied openings within the screen filter the light into shifting patterns on the interior surfaces," Taylor says. "At night, when the lights are on, the effect is reversed and the cabin glows like a lantern."

SPECIAL FEATURES FOR THIS PLAN

- BUILT OFF-SITE AND THEN REASSEMBLED AT THE LAKE, A METHOD THAT SIGNIFICANTLY REDUCED COSTS AND THE DURATION OF CONSTRUCTION
- CEDAR SLAT PRIVACY SIDING ARRANGED IN AN EYE-CATCHING PATTERN
- GREEN ROOF FOR ENHANCED ENERGY EFFICIENCY AND TO BLEND THE STRUCTURE INTO THE LANDSCAPE

Structurally, the cabin is a box with three walls of floor-to-ceiling glass wrapped with the screen which, in addition to its aesthetic qualities, performs another important role: the owners can see out but their guests can't see in. Another bonus is that the screen shades and helps to stabilize the building. Inside, the bed is flanked by storage cabinets and the birch plywood surfaces reveal the inherent beauty of a modest product. The floor extends outside toward the lake to become a deck with access to an outdoor shower, also enclosed by a cedar screen.

The construction of the cabin took an unusual twist at the prompting of the husband, who is experienced in building and wanted to stage an experiment of sorts. The cabin was preassembled in a Toronto parking lot, where every detail could be overseen and perfected. This method was cost-effective and quick: a team of furniture craftsmen built the cabin in just four weeks. The components of the cabin were then numbered, disassembled and reconstructed on-site in just ten days. "We were able to reduce

costs by an estimated 30 percent by decreasing construction time and simplifying the difficulties of working at a remote site," Taylor points out.

The owners also wanted to incorporate environmentally responsible features into the cabin, and that goal was accomplished with a green roof that raised the R-value of the roof and gives the uphill neighbors a pleasant view of foliage instead of a solid mass. In addition, doors at each end of the cabin capitalize on lake breezes to provide cross ventilation.

In the end, everyone is happy. The sleeping cabin gets near year-round use, guests can come and go as they please, and the owners have a new appreciation for the place they've loved for more than two decades. "We wanted a contemporary building," the wife says. "And we wanted to experience the site in a different way. The cabin has given us a whole new perspective on being at the lake."

1 The cabin sits lightly on the land on a base of steel beams supported by concrete caissons, a construction technique that minimized disruption to the site. The building itself is a glass box wrapped on three sides by a cedar slat privacy screen that over time will gray into a soft silver color. Although they appear to be ran-

domly placed, the slats were painstakingly arranged before the start of construction.

2 A narrow opening in the screen frames a section of the view. Although the cabin has a transparent look and feel, the screen insures privacy on the sides of the building visible from the main cottage.

3 The cabin was built in a Toronto parking lot, disassembled, and then shipped to the site in numbered pieces for reassembly, which took just ten days. This method slashed the budget by 30 percent and cut construction time to just over five weeks.

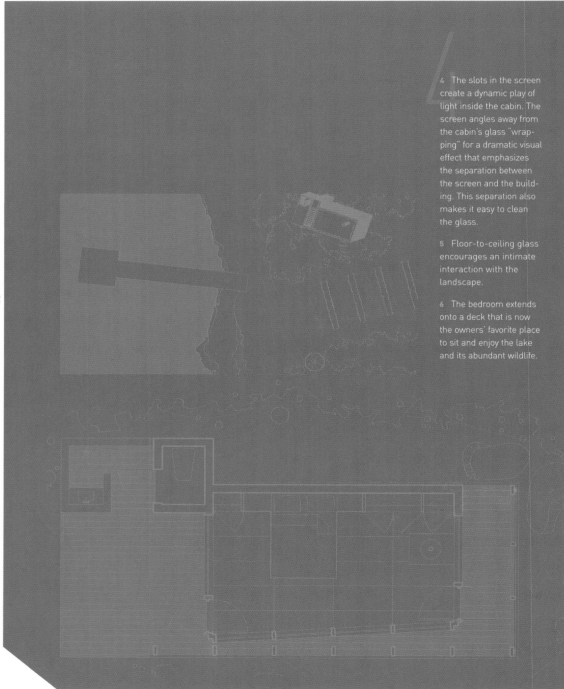

4 The slots in the screen create a dynamic play of light inside the cabin. The screen angles away from the cabin's glass "wrapping" for a dramatic visual effect that emphasizes the separation between the screen and the building. This separation also makes it easy to clean the glass.

5 Floor-to-ceiling glass encourages an intimate interaction with the landscape.

6 The bedroom extends onto a deck that is now the owners' favorite place to sit and enjoy the lake and its abundant wildlife.

7   The bedroom has plenty of built-in storage and spectacular views of the lake thanks to a large cutout in the screen. The monochromatic interior palette of birch veneer plywood coated with a polyurethane finish is a refined complement to the exterior cedar.

8   The entry forms a small partially enclosed porch.

9   The roof of the cabin extends over the deck in a series of open beams. The architect chose untreated cedar for the exterior because of its weather-resistant properties and beautiful color.

Little appears to separate the living room, clearly visible on the west side of the cabin, from its ranch setting; in fact, the effect is of an open space. This desired transparency was achieved with a glass frame supported by structural steel beams that hold the building together and make it resistant to high winds and even tornadoes. By suspending the second-level deck from the roof, the architect was able to partially shelter the patio below.

the transparent house

DESIGN: JAY HARGRAVE, COTTAM HARGRAVE

PHOTOGRAPHS: PATRICK WONG

LOCATION: GEORGETOWN, TEXAS   1,000 SQUARE FEET

This striking cabin is an extreme example of connecting a house to its site. With a façade that all but disappears into the landscape, the building reveals what can be done when privacy isn't an issue and embarking on an architectural adventure isn't just a passing notion but practically a request.

"This project represented an opportunity to build without many of the constraints one is faced with in typical situations," says architect Jay Hargrave. "The owner wanted to build a piece of art on his 1,800-acre ranch. He saw this is as a special piece of property [as of this writing, it was in the process of being converted into an environmental land bank], and he wanted the house to take a backseat to the land. The house fades away in some respects, leaving the landscape as the focus."

The cabin's oversized roof and exposed inner workings give the impression of an exotic winged creature perched on the ground. The 1,000-square-foot structure elegantly meets the needs of its single owner, who expressly did not want separate rooms, walls or window coverings. The goal, Hargrave says, was an open-plan house that would give the occupant the exhilaration of being outdoors—but with the added perk of being sheltered from the elements. To achieve this, the architect took the concept of transparency and raised it to an exaggerated level: the interiors are visible at every elevation—even the bathroom has no doors or coverings. ("The owner tells me this keeps guests from staying too long," Hargrave quips.)

SPECIAL FEATURES FOR THIS PLAN

- GLASS BOX THAT REVEALS THE BONES OF THE BUILDING AND FOSTERS A STRONG VISUAL AND PHYSICAL CONNECTION TO THE SETTING

- STABILIZED WITH A BRICK CORE THAT PREVENTS THE BUILDING FROM COLLAPSING AND ACTS AS A CENTERPIECE WITHIN THE EXPOSED INTERIOR

2

A streamlined materials palette kept the lines of the building clean and the interiors visually consistent. Hargrave used tongue-and-groove cedar for the roof deck, sealed and waxed concrete for the interior floors, honed limestone for the counters and steel for the spiral stair.

1 Eight-foot overhangs on the standing seam copper roof effectively shield the interiors from the sun. The brick core provides crucial lateral bracing; is an enclosure for the HVAC and plumbing systems; serves as a backdrop for a kitchenette, reading nook, and three fireplaces; and in one area morphs into a staircase that leads to a rooftop deck.

2 The bedroom was placed on the east side of the cabin to allow the owner to wake up with the sun. The upper level of the house has a study with a reading nook set into the brick core.

3 The primary exterior materials are glass, brick, steel and limestone. An outdoor shower just off the bathroom brings the owner into even closer contact with nature.

The cabin, a 20x40x18 glass box supported with steel braces, is relatively straightforward in form but its fabrication was a complex process. "Because the house is all bones, craft was important from the very beginning," the architect notes. The building is intersected by an eight-foot-thick brick core; structurally the core prevents the house from folding in on itself and, in a home where nothing is hidden, it provided a solution to where to put the HVAC and plumbing systems. The core also contains a kitchenette, three fireplaces, an upstairs reading nook and storage closets.

Hargrave acknowledges that building a glass house in Texas might seem like a bad idea. Blistering temperatures could ostensibly bake the occupants, but eight-foot overhangs shield the interiors from sunlight and minimize solar gain on the windows. In addition, the floor plan works with the path of the sun to keep the owner cool even during the height of summer: the bedroom was placed on

3

the east side of the building so that he can wake up to the sun. As the sun begins its journey across the sky and the temperatures rise, the owner can move to the living room, still in shade, and so forth. As dusk approaches, he can move up to the roof deck to watch the sunset.

4 Spiral staircases work well in small rooms because they don't encroach on living space. The stair terminates at a catwalk, which in turn leads to the rooftop deck. The concrete floors were stained black and then sealed and waxed to an ebony-like sheen.

5 The living room is furnished with modern couches and chairs and has very little ornamentation, the one exception a whimsical glass light fixture adorned with polka dots. The owner had no need for a full kitchen; instead he requested a no-frills kitchenette. Limestone lintels add a bright accent to the room.

North

South

East

West

6

6   The streamlined bathroom, which has a hammered copper sink and a limestone counter, is built into the brick core.

7   Sliding glass doors open the bedroom to the patio. The owner eschewed window coverings, preferring instead to enjoy unimpeded views of the ranch.

8   Three portals in the recessed reading nook, located in the upstairs study, provide views down into the living room. The fireplace has a limestone hearth supported by steel legs.

9   Hallways cut into the brick core help direct navigation through the cabin, and arches soften the bold horizontal and vertical lines of the design. The floor and ceiling are cedar and the railing is steel.

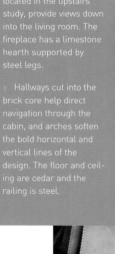

7

8

9

A basic cube built on a tight budget, the Black Box shows what can be achieved with an imaginative approach to common off-the-shelf materials, including Douglas fir, perforated metal and Baltic birch plywood. The cabin is designed for flexibility: it can be used as an office, den or guest room. The landscape of rock, gravel, succulents, and birch and magnolia trees is low maintenance and drought-resistant.

black **box**

DESIGN: PATRICK TIGHE, TIGHE ARCHITECTURE

PHOTOGRAPHS: ART GRAY

LOCATION: SANTA MONICA, CALIFORNIA   225 SQUARE FEET

This little building looks like a cabin in the woods but that's where the comparison ends. The setting is the bustling city of Santa Monica, seven blocks from the Pacific Ocean.

The work of an enterprising young architect who wanted a multifunctional guest room/office/den, the one-room, 225-square-foot cabin, affectionately called the Black Box, has garnered Patrick Tighe awards for its affordable design and strong architectural aesthetic. Armed with a budget of just $20,000, Tighe explored ways to experiment with materials and apply sophisticated lines and details while keeping the construction program low-tech. "It's not a complicated building in any way," he says. "The objective from the beginning was to figure out how to take a simple box and a very low budget and create some kind of architecture—to be inventive with materials and playful with the composition of windows and doors."

Tighe was careful to give the Black Box a sense of warmth and containment, attributes crucial to any cabin, regardless of locale. That was achieved with lots of wood inside and perforated metal privacy screens outside that, when pulled across the windows, permit dappled light to shine into the room and prevent passersby from seeing in. He introduced contrast by complementing the rough wood siding with smooth, light-colored Baltic birch plywood on the ceiling and floor. The siding, vertical strips of recycled Douglas fir finished with a dark stain and placed over an asphalt-shingle skin attached to the framing, makes a statement without

SPECIAL FEATURES FOR THIS PLAN

- CABIN STYLE IN THE MIDDLE OF A BUSY URBAN NEIGHBORHOOD

- BUILT ON A LIMITED BUDGET USING RECYCLED WOOD AND WINDOWS AND COMMON OFF-THE-SHELF MATERIALS

being too bold for the neighborhood. Inside, the horizontal placement of the plywood makes the room feel spacious.

Tighe acknowledges that finding ways to maximize the square footage was high on his list of priorities. His solutions included leaving the ceiling framing exposed in order to tap into the height of the room and using built-ins instead of regular furniture; as a result, the room easily accommodates a combined couch/bed, desk and perimeter shelving.

The Black Box was a mere four months in the making, proving that a retreat, whether urban or rural, can be completed in a short amount of time—which means the occupants can get down to the business of enjoying a bit of quiet time.

1 The 225-square-foot cabin is connected to the main house by a deck made from recycled Douglas fir planks stained the same color as the siding. The deck separates the cabin from the house but keeps it close for easy access.

2 The exterior reveals an eye-catching arrangement of materials—all of them off-the-shelf but used in ways that make them appear anything but ordinary.

3 Low-cost perforated metal privacy screens obscure views into the cabin without blocking sunlight. The screens slide on inexpensive industrial track hardware.

4 Built-ins make the most of any small room. A desk tucked into a corner and connected on one side to a couch/ bed is a practical addition that doesn't take up valuable space. The sliding glass door can be opened to ventilate the room and connect it to the garden and, if desired, the perforated metal screen can be pulled across the opening.

5 The cabin is warm and inviting thanks to the use of cedar for the walls and Baltic birch plywood for the ceiling and floor. (Although plywood is not the most durable flooring for high-traffic zones, it works well in rooms where less activity is anticipated.) The coffee table is the architect's original design: he placed a square of resin on a steel frame to make a budget-friendly piece of custom furniture. A built-in combination couch/bed runs the length of the room and then turns a corner to continue on another wall. Leaving the ceiling exposed made it possible to maximize the height of the room.

6 By placing the desk right up against the corner window, the architect made sure that anyone working in the room would enjoy a direct experience with nature.

7 The architect created an interesting visual effect using just a few materials. The siding is strips of recycled Douglas fir placed against a skin of black asphalt shingles attached to the framing.

6

7

solid as **a rock**

DESIGN: DAN MOLENAAR, MAFCO HOUSE

PHOTOGRAPHS: JOSEPH FRANKE AND CHRISTOPHER WADSWORTH

LOCATION: DRAG LAKE, HALIBURTON, ONTARIO   900 SQUARE FEET

Dan and Diane Molenaar of Toronto had a vision for their weekend cabin and they were willing to go beyond all forms of tradition—and agree to a bit of roughing it—to realize their dream.

The journey began with a search for a site. The perfect place would be removed from city life but within reasonable driving distance. Ideally it would be an unoccupied length of shoreline on a deep, crystal-clear lake, a parcel of land carpeted in thick stands of trees and positioned to capture the solar properties of southern exposure. As luck would have it, the couple heard about such a property at Drag Lake, a popular vacation spot about two hours' drive from Toronto. Upon learning that the six-and-a-half-acre lot had no road (boat access or, in winter, walking across the ice, would be the only way in) and was perched above the lake on a cliff-like rocky outcropping, the Molenaars were sold. "It had been too extreme for the person who had looked at it before us," Dan says. "But it appealed to Diane and me right away."

Beauty and solitude aside, the site came with a number of potential setbacks. In addition to the lack of a road, it had no electricity and no drinking water supply. These facts didn't faze the Molenaars. Says Dan, "We knew we were up for the challenges, and I had spent a lot of time as a teenager camping in the backcountry, so living off the grid didn't worry me."

SPECIAL FEATURES FOR THIS PLAN

- OFF-THE-GRID GETAWAY ACCESSIBLE ONLY BY WATER AND SUPPORTED BY SOLAR-POWERED ENERGY AND PROPANE APPLIANCES
- WINDOWS SALVAGED FROM CITY OFFICE TOWERS
- BARE-BONES AMENITIES EXCEPT FOR IN THE KITCHEN, WHICH IS EQUIPPED WITH A GOURMET RANGE THAT HAS BEEN CONVERTED TO PROPANE

1 The cabin's heavy-duty sliding entry door expands to a width of ten feet. Reclaimed glass was used here and for the windows. Photo by Joseph Franke.

The couple then embarked on another adventure: to design and build the cabin themselves. Dan had some experience—he had worked as a carpenter and taken college-level architecture courses. Also, the couple shared a passion for mid-century design and, in particular, Frank Lloyd Wright's flat-roofed Usonian houses of the 1930s and 1940s. Using Wright as their inspiration, the Molenaars drew up the plans for their cabin, which they named Barerock. They had specific goals: create a retreat that would exist harmoniously with the setting and sit lightly on the land; use natural and, if possible, salvaged materials; and make do with a no-frills layout free of interior dividing walls and wrapped in a glass skin to maximize warmth from the sun and blur the line between inside and out. "We wanted a simple structure that grew out of the topography, with only a few citified comforts," Dan explains. "Our friends talk about their time at the cabin as five-star camping and primitive elegance."

There was another factor too: budget. In the end, thanks to their hands-on approach and commitment to low-cost materials, the Molenaars built Barerock over the course of two years for a very reasonable $165,000.

The 900-square-foot post-and-beam structure sits low to the ground on concrete piers; using piers instead of a foundation prevented damage to the natural drainage patterns on the site. The exterior is clad in bronze-colored aluminum composite panels that help blend the building into the forest. To keep the cabin low maintenance, the Molenaars used techniques and materials that would require minimal upkeep over the years—for example, the flat roof has been structurally engineered to withstand local snow loads and is sealed with a long-lasting rubber membrane. Barerock is equipped with an on-demand propane water heater, a propane refrigerator and a gourmet range that has been converted from natural gas to propane. (The range ended up being the one extravagance Dan and Diane, both avid cooks, allowed themselves.) Water is pumped up from the lake and stored in a sixty-five-gallon pressurized tank.

The Molenaars wanted large windows on the cabin, both to frame the views and welcome the warming sun (the cabin's primary heat sources are two wood-burning stoves). The glazing, in fact, has an interesting story: one day the couple tuned into a radio show about a recycling company that was in the process of reclaiming 4,000 units of highly reflective window glass from a pair of Toronto office towers. Says Dan, "The thought of taking glass that office workers had viewed the city through and setting it down in the middle of the woods had an irresistible whimsy to it, not to mention a certain budgetary appeal." The couple hurried to purchase forty units.

Construction was an arduous but ultimately rewarding experience. Dan enlisted his grown son and friends to haul the materials to the site—with no road access, everything had to be loaded onto a boat, transported across the lake, and then lugged up the cliff to the site. In total, Dan and his volunteer workers hand-carried 164 sixty-pound sacks of concrete, two woodstoves, a stove, all the windows (each of which weighs ninety pounds), and a set of Douglas fir framing beams.

The work now behind them and the opportunities for relaxation stretched enticingly before them, the Molenaars are pleased with the result of their effort. The cabin, basic but comfortable even during the frigid Canadian winters, provides the respite they craved. And, their sense of self-reliance has grown in the knowledge that Barerock can function on its own.

"There is a feeling of freedom and independence from the grid," Dan reflects. "We feel that the house is a symbolic divider between the world of mechanized convenience we take for granted and the wilderness."

2 The owner designed and built the communal dining table and matching benches from padauk, an African hardwood. The table extends from the kitchen island in a configuration that keeps those seated in contact with the cook. The ten-foot opening made by pulling back the sliding glass doors ventilates the room in the hot summer months. Photo by Joseph Franke.

3 A steel cross-bracing system provides lateral support to the building in the absence of shear walls. Photo by Joseph Franke.

2

4 Perched seventy feet above the lake in a stand of trees, the cabin rests on a low-impact concrete pier base. The building's low-slung horizontal design and glass skin encourage a dramatic interaction between the house and its untamed setting. Photo by Christopher Wadsworth.

5 The couple found their dream site—850 feet of rocky shoreline—at Drag Lake, a popular getaway about two hours from Toronto. The terrain is characterized by thick stands of white pine and oak trees, some of them old-growth. The only access to the six-and-a-half-acre property is by boat or by walking across the ice during the winter. Photo by Christopher Wadsworth.

6 The cabin is clad in maintenance-free anodized aluminum panels in a bronze that resembles the bark of the surrounding trees. The remoteness of the area and the lack of a road meant everything had to be done by hand—even the materials and appliances had to be carried up from the lake. Highly reflective reclaimed office tower windows were a budget-friendly and long-lasting choice, and they veil the interior by mirroring the trees. Photo by Christopher Wadsworth.

7 The scenery is reflected back in the glass. The alignment of two sets of sliding glass doors—one at the entry, another parallel to the dining table—creates a see-through breezeway when both doors are open. Photo by Christopher Wadsworth.

6

7

We feel that the house is a symbolic divider between the world of mechanized convenience we take for granted and the wilderness.

8 A mirror above the kitchen cabinets fosters the illusion of a larger space. Appliances include a stainless steel gas range converted to propane and a propane refrigerator. Photo by Joseph Franke.

9 The bedroom at the far end of the cabin is separated from the kitchen by an enclosed bathroom. Photo by Christopher Wadsworth.

10 The interior materials are unpretentious and affordable. The panel flooring is Douglas fir plywood stained a cherry bark color and treated with a high-pigment urethane to improve durability. Douglas fir was also used on the ceiling and for the window frames, which were custom-milled to fit the reclaimed glazing. Even though temperatures can drop well below freezing in the winter, two wood-burning stoves keep the cabin comfortable. The reflective glass allows the owners' dog, Nigel, to spy on deer walking past the cabin; he can see them but they can't see him. Photo by Christopher Wadsworth.

9

10

city style in the **mountains**

DESIGN: STEPHEN DYNIA, STEPHEN DYNIA ARCHITECTS
PHOTOGRAPHS: ROGER WADE AND CAMERON NEILSON
LOCATION: JACKSON, WYOMING   2,300 SQUARE FEET

This Jackson getaway has something of a split personality: outside it's a solid-looking mountain cabin wedged into a narrow alley in a neighborhood of sheet metal buildings and sheds. Inside, it's a sleek loft-style space filled with contemporary materials and refined details and finishes.

Architect Stephen Dynia, whose stamp can be found on many homes in Jackson and the surrounding area, did not happen upon this effect by chance. A proponent of the importance of context in residential architecture, he allowed the site to dictate the design.

"The cabin pays homage to the town's alleys, which are filled with remnants from another era," Dynia says. "Those tiny cabins and sheds are part of Jackson's history, and I didn't want to come in and do a house that would try to take that over. It had to fit the theme of the community."

The owner, a part-time resident who retreats to Jackson to ski in winter and hike in summer, owns two city lots; one of those was already occupied by a tiny log cabin, which Dynia remodeled into a guest house. The new cabin's building envelope—long

SPECIAL FEATURES FOR THIS PLAN

- RUGGED OUTSIDE AND SOPHISTICATED INSIDE, A DESIGN SOLUTION THAT MET THE REQUIREMENTS OF BOTH THE NEIGHBORHOOD AND THE OWNER

- ROOFTOP DECK THAT FEELS LIKE AN OUTDOOR ROOM AND IS CONNECTED TO THE CABIN WITH DIRECT INDOOR/OUTDOOR ACCESS

- CURVED INTERIOR WALL THAT SERVES AS A FOCAL POINT AND HELPS DIVIDE THE SPACES BY FUNCTION

2

1 Pulling back the sliding glass doors at the living room links the space to a rooftop deck, located over the garage on the south end of the house. The soffit is marine-grade maple plywood to match the interior ceiling. Photo by Cameron Neilson.

2 A stair on the east façade connects the roof deck to the yard. A band of windows on the second story visually defines the primary living level and keeps the space filled with natural light without sacrificing privacy. The architect chose a long-lasting standing seam rusted metal roof. Photo by Roger Wade.

and narrow and bisected by alleys—was a familiar scenario to Dynia. He says, "We were dealing with an urban-type lot, but in a mountain town. The challenge was to open the house to the landscape even in this crowded area, and give the owner great views without losing privacy."

The cabin's exterior features a carefully arranged selection of materials that give it an edge without turning it flashy. Horizontal and vertical cedar siding, rusted steel and stucco together give the façade the desired rustic appearance—but with a few modern touches to hint at what's inside. In addition to keeping the building rooted to its setting, these materials are durable enough for Jackson's famously variable weather: dry and hot in summer, damp and cold in winter. A stair at the east elevation leads to a roof deck that functions as a partially sheltered—and private—outdoor room through all the seasons. A long band of windows, also on the east side, ensures that the interiors are consistently filled with natural light and, due to their second-floor position, are high enough off the ground to block views into the house.

Inside, the story changes altogether. Gone is the toned-down, earthy palette, replaced with an urban sensibility and the playful use of color. Dynia arranged the spaces in a way that provides zones of privacy in an otherwise open floor plan. As an example, the owner's combination bedroom/yoga studio is connected to the rest of the house visually, but Dynia raised it three and a half feet above the living room to allow it to stand apart. Interior materials include maple plywood, Brazilian ipe, stained concrete, stainless steel and perforated metal. The second-level living room opens to the roof deck through wide sliding glass doors, an orientation that makes it possible to quickly expand the dimensions of the room in agreeable weather.

Several details warrant special mention: a curved plaster wall painted a vivid shade of blue, which defines the individual spaces; a buoyant ceiling of maple plywood panels accentuated with black reveals and supported with steel tie rods; and a small kitchen built into the plaster wall.

"This has become the owner's special place," Dynia reflects. "It's quiet, comfortable, and every part of the cabin works for his lifestyle."

3 The cabin's dramatic atrium-style entry hall reveals how a variety of materials can be used to create a sophisticated design. The light-colored maple plywood ceiling, with its dark reveals and elegant tie-rod truss system, visually raises the ceiling and acts like a large light fixture: sunlight bounces off the panels, imbuing the space with a soft glow. Because the cabin has few full interior walls, the curved wall served the key purpose of helping divide the rooms. Photo by Roger Wade.

SECTIONS

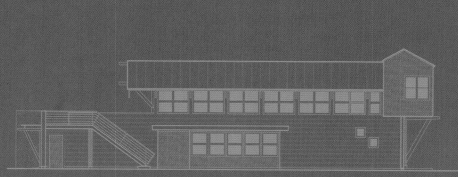

EAST

NORTH

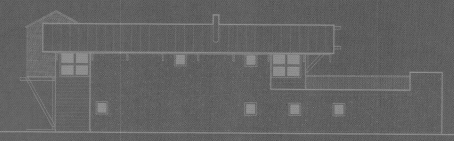

SOUTH

WEST

UPPER FLOOR PLAN

Deck

Office

Dressing Room

Bathroom | Bathroom

Bedroom

MAIN FLOOR PLAN

Garage

Mudroom

Mechanical Room

Living Room

Dining Room

Kitchen

Pantry

Powder Room

Entry

0   5'   10'   20'

Deck

Main House

Patio

4 The kitchen is tucked into a section of the curved wall to give it a feeling of enclosure and intimacy without walls or doors. Maple plywood cabinets match the ceiling, and stainless steel counters and a perforated metal ceiling give the space a streamlined appearance. Photo by Roger Wade.

5 A prefab wood-burning fireplace set into the wall becomes the focal point of a casual sitting area on the first floor. Built-in maple plywood cabinets provide storage, and logs can be stacked on either side of the unit. Photo by Roger Wade.

6 The stair mimics the placement of the exterior roof deck stair, and the curved plaster wall divides the kitchen from the entry hall. Concrete floors are a wise choice for mountain environments because they resist stains and can be easily cleaned. Photo by Roger Wade.

7 Styled like a loft, the living room features crisp white walls and dark Brazilian ipe floors. The room continues onto a roof deck. Photo by Roger Wade.

8 The owner wanted a special room that he could use for yoga and meditation or as an extra bedroom (the couch folds out into a bed). The architect raised the room three and a half feet above the second floor to keep it independent of the other spaces without closing it off completely. The ceiling of the room is perforated metal and the wall edge is clad in rusted steel. Photo by Roger Wade.

8

The 768-square-foot cabin is clad in cold-rolled corrugated steel that was sprayed repeatedly with saltwater to accelerate the rusting process and achieve a dark sepia tone, which the architect felt would harmonize with the native trees and river rocks. The rusting process took only ten days and cost very little. The large window at the living room lowers at the push of a button and stops at railing height to form a twenty-four-inch-wide counter.

a river runs **under it**

DESIGN: RON MASON, ANDERSON MASON DALE ARCHITECTS

PHOTOGRAPHS: RON MASON

LOCATION: BUENA VISTA, COLORADO   768 SQUARE FEET

Architect Ron Mason would probably admit he's a romantic, but he would just as likely temper that description with a healthy dose of practicality. Yes, his cabin on the banks of the Arkansas River pulls at his heartstrings every time he thinks about it. Yes, he thinks often of the river itself, whose rapids he has navigated by kayak hundreds of times. Yes, he thinks back to the Ute Indians encamped on the land, which was later divided into mining claims. And yes, when the rest of the buildings at his mountain compound become filled with visiting children, grandchildren and friends, a place of his own makes all the difference.

The "Tube," as Mason calls it, is one of seven buildings on this seventeen-acre property near the town of Buena Vista. "It's a spectacular spot, and even before I owned it I thought it would be wonderful to build there," Mason says. "I've had a long-standing romance with rivers, especially the Arkansas."

Mason, who lives and works in Denver, began to realize his dream of a whitewater getaway when he purchased the land for $14,000 in 1973. In addition to the Tube, the compound includes a lodge-style main cabin for family gatherings, a guest cabin, an observation/meditation/sleeping tower, a studio, a workshop and a teepee. The Tube was meant to be a caretaker's unit but as construction progressed Mason found it hard to resist the temptation to claim the cabin for himself and his partner Gillian

1

SPECIAL FEATURES FOR THIS PLAN

■ INNOVATIVE DESIGN THAT CANTILEVERS HALF THE BUILDING OVER THE RIVER FOR A TRULY DIRECT EXPERIENCE WITH THE SETTING

■ LARGE ORANGE-MULLIONED WINDOW THAT CAN BE RETRACTED AT THE TOUCH OF A BUTTON TO FORM A GLASS RAILING AND COUNTER

2

1 A tight building envelope with little room for expansion required a think-out-of-the-box approach. The cabin appears to float above the river but is supported by a steel truss system that allows half the forty-eight-foot-long structure to cantilever over the water, a design that gracefully adapted to the constraints of the site. This aesthetic balancing act also conformed to the architect's goal of treading as lightly as possible on the land.

2 The Tube was envisioned as a sort of telescope, with the window serving as a lens that focuses the views toward the river. The only color in the room is the window frame, painted International Orange for a bright contrast against the muted tones of the Southern yellow pine walls, ceiling and floor.

Johnson, an interior designer. In the end, that temptation proved stronger than his original intentions and the cabin became a personal retreat.

Whitewater dreams aside, Mason faced two potentially discouraging challenges, one put in place by Mother Nature herself and another by federal land management agencies: the available building site was constrained by physical obstacles (large boulders and a sharp bend in the river) and government easements that had been instituted years before. "The Tube's placement and design were entirely dictated by the site," he says.

"There wasn't much else I could do but build a very narrow cabin and allow half of it to hang out in space." Mason isn't exaggerating: the Tube is forty-eight feet long, twenty-four of which are thrust out over the river. It might sound precarious but the architect encased the cabin in a sturdy framework of steel trusses to stabilize the building and ensure that it will stay put.

The 768-square-foot cabin is modest in size but comfortable. An open living room and kitchen and a separate bedroom and bathroom were all Mason desired, and he chose a neutral materials palette for the sake of simplicity and consistency. The primary interior material is tongue-and-groove yellow pine, used for the walls, ceiling and floors; outside, rusted steel siding pulls the cabin into the landscape. The only color

is found at the large window at the end of the living room; Mason painted its mullions a bright orange to draw attention to the window and the views beyond. The window can be retracted at the touch of a button; in its lowered position it forms a glass railing and a twenty-four-inch-wide counter. "It's amazing to be in this room because you are attracted to the window right away. Its purpose is to act like a lens to focus everything inside out toward the river," he explains. "It facilitates a compelling and very powerful encounter with nature."

3 The window takes the view from eye-catching to unforgettable. The counter formed by lowering the window can be used as an informal dining table or a place to stand and enjoy the scenery.

4 Almost ship-like in its presentation and layout, the cabin is small but feels spacious as a result of the architect's selection of light-colored materials and generous use of glass.

The Tube

ARKANSAS RIVER

SITE PLAN

The central axis of the Tube is aimed down the river valley and affords a spectacular view of its rapids and surrounding landscape.

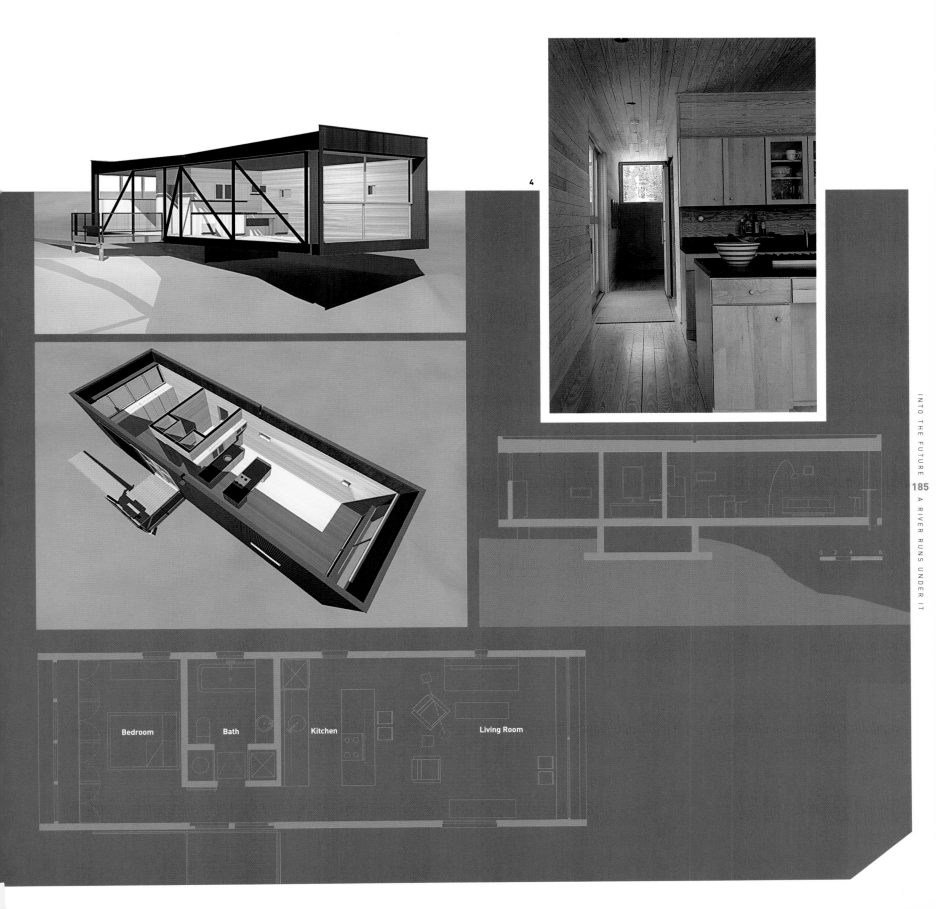

Bedroom   **Bath**   **Kitchen**   **Living Room**

0 2 4   8

5 Southern yellow pine siding and a redwood entry platform bring subtle variation to the pared-down materials palette. A band of windows at the bedroom permits light inside without compromising privacy.

6 The bedroom looks out onto 500-foot cliffs and stays tidy thanks to storage closets built into the wall below the windows.

7 The kitchen is small but functional. Maple cabinets and plastic laminate counters complement the Southern yellow pine used elsewhere in the cabin.

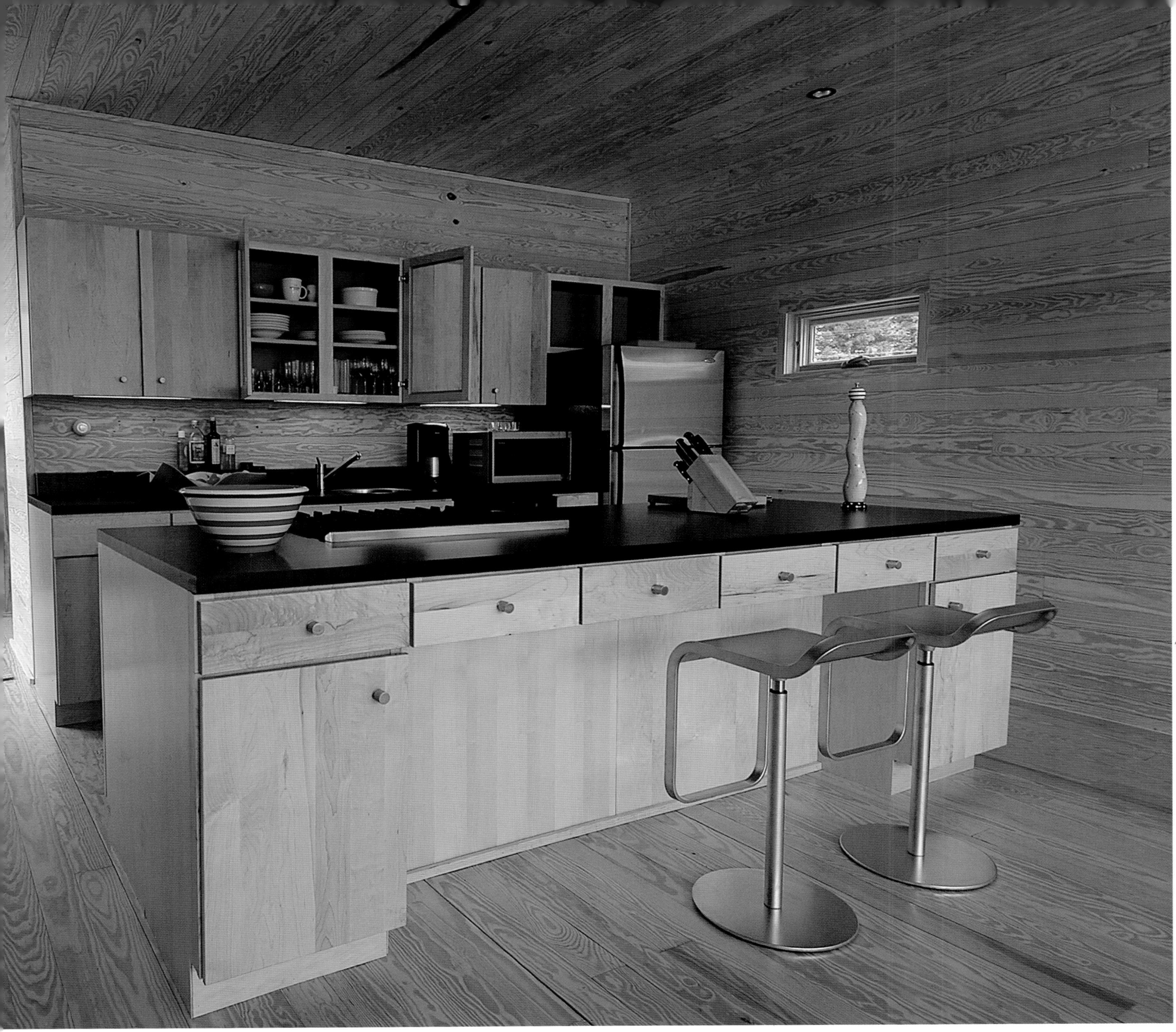

The main living shelf swings off the two-story base in a dramatic cantilever that extends the cabin into the tree canopy, and a catwalk with bar-grating enhances the home's interaction with the setting. Exterior materials were chosen for durability and beauty; they include vertical tongue-and-groove cedar with a natural stain (cantilevered portion), cedar plywood with a gray-green stain (base) and galvanized steel. The low-maintenance siding only has to be retouched every five to six years.

high-tech **lake house**

DESIGN: ERIC COBB, E. COBB ARCHITECTURE, INC.
PHOTOGRAPHS: STEVE KEATING
LOCATION: WENATCHEE, WASHINGTON   3,200 SQUARE FEET

This lakeside cabin for an educational software developer/teacher couple and their young children might just be the perfect getaway. Kids love its nooks and crannies and spacious play areas and people of all ages will appreciate its family-focused plan, durable and beautiful materials, proximity to outdoor activities and smart-house technology that makes the home run like a well-oiled machine.

The home was designed by Eric Cobb, who took a difficult site on a lake in the Cascade Mountain range and used it to its best advantage. Perched near a cliff, the rectangular and steeply sloped site is accessed by a narrow gravel driveway that feeds two other properties. The architect responded to this shared access by positioning the garage adjacent to the driveway and as far down the slope and as close to the lake as possible. To minimize excavation and preserve trees (in fact, only one tree had to be removed during construction, and it happened to be dead), Cobb arranged the home's main components—a top box, a slender two-story base and a cantilevered shelf balanced between the two—according to the contours of the land, stepping the pieces down the site and poising them delicately in the tree canopy in a configuration that promotes an intimate encounter with the environment and results in a functional exterior and interior layout suited to active outdoor life and the entertaining of lots of guests.

SPECIAL FEATURES FOR THIS PLAN

- ■ "SMART HOUSE" FEATURES, INCLUDING AN ELECTRIC SNOW MELT SYSTEM AND WEB CAMERAS THAT TRACK SNOW ACCUMULATION, ALLOWING THE CABIN TO BE MONITORED WHILE UNOCCUPIED

- ■ KID-FRIENDLY DESIGN COMPLETE WITH CLIMBING WALL, CHALKBOARD WALL AND HIDDEN PASSAGES BETWEEN SLEEPING BUNKS

1 The base of the house is a bunk room/play area with built-in daybeds and plenty of room on the floor for futon mattresses. The climbing wall connects to an upper-level bunk chamber, which allows the kids to reach their sleeping quarters without using the stairs.

2 A chalkboard wall supports the stair, which winds through the center of the house, joining the three floors. The flooring in this high-use part of the house is end-grain Douglas fir with a varied color that helps disguise dings and scratches. The chalkboard wall is a practical message center and an outlet for artistic expression.

These three discrete elements give the owners a variety of ways to interact with the building and the landscape. The top box contains a two-car garage with a mudroom, elevator and below-grade storage; an outdoor stair terminates at the main entry, which is tucked into the space between the box and the shelf. The base, with its four bedrooms, bunk cabin, built-in daybeds, built-in half bunk and two bathrooms, provides comfortable sleeping quarters for up to twelve people. Using the base as its platform, the shelf swings off at a radical cantilever, orienting the main living area views toward the lake and the mountains beyond. "Locking the base and the garage into the site allowed the third component, the cantilevered section, to be special and different," the architect points out.

Cobb continued his creativity inside with a floor plan tailored for kids of all ages; a climbing wall, chalkboard wall and hidden passages between sleeping quarters turn the house into an indoor playground. Interior materials were chosen for their aesthetic appeal and durability and include maple veneer plywood, Douglas fir and glass.

The owners, who live in Seattle, also wanted a way to monitor the cabin from a distance, and this is where the smarthouse technology comes in. Features include an electric snow melt system that prevents drifts from blocking the garage and deck doors and the path to the hot tub. Two Web cameras train their electronic eyes on parts of the house where snow accumulation could become problematic if unattended, alerting the owners to any glitches in the snow melt system. Interior and exterior lights are set on individual controls, and a signal indicates when any windows or doors are open.

Cobb believes the cabin works on many levels—it is low-maintenance, can gracefully accommodate high-energy family life and houseguests, and is connected to its setting in a way that keeps the occupants in close contact with nature at all times. "The typical mountain cabin experience can often be about the indoors," he says. "But this house pays equal attention to the outdoors. I like to think it coexists with the land, and that relationship really strengthens the bond between the people in the cabin and the natural world around them."

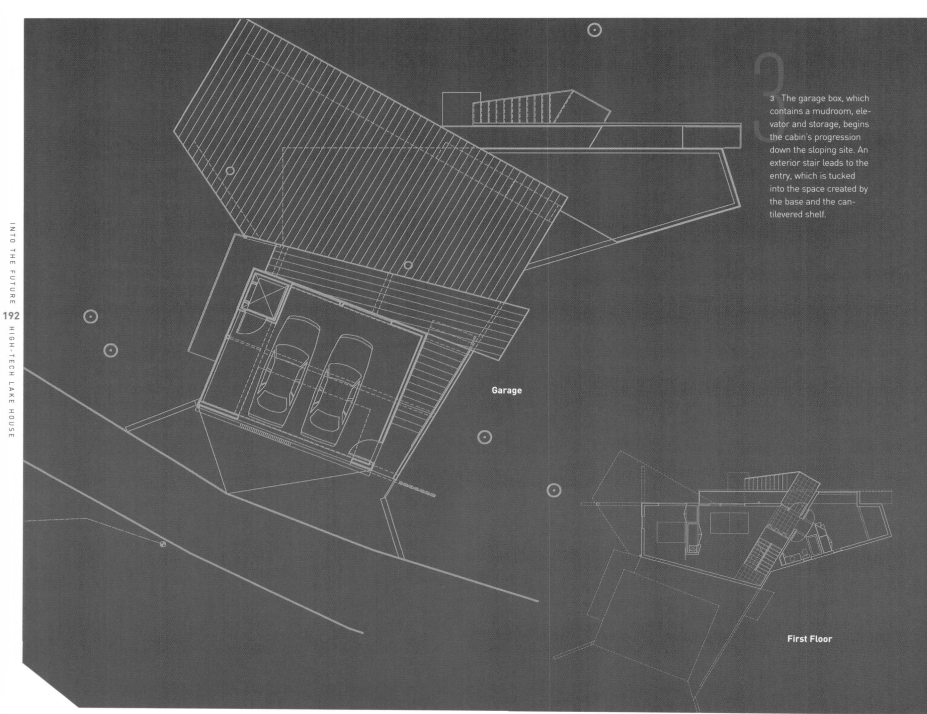

3 The garage box, which contains a mudroom, elevator and storage, begins the cabin's progression down the sloping site. An exterior stair leads to the entry, which is tucked into the space created by the base and the cantilevered shelf.

Garage

First Floor

3

Second Floor

Living Room

Kitchen

Dining

Roof Deck

Hot Tub

Mudroom

Storage

Third Floor

4

4 The stair is central to the interior design. The chalkboard wall anchors it on one side, and clear tempered glass panels held together with custom steel clips are separated at junctures with a steel guard rail. The treads are glulam and the floor on this level is maple.

5 Two islands with maple butcher block counters run parallel to each other to form a galley kitchen in the cantilevered shelf, which also accommodates a living room and dining area. Exterior cameras monitor snow accumulation, and an electric snow melt system keeps the doors and walkways clear of drifts.

6 The cabin's precise design is revealed in one of the bathrooms, where drawers fit perfectly into the angular geometry of the room. The cabinetry is maple veneer plywood and the counter and sink are stainless steel.

5

I like to think that the house coexists with the land, and that **relationship really strengthens the bond** between the people in the cabin and the natural world around them.

7 The maple veneer plywood bunk chamber, one of two in the house, is compact and cozy. The chamber is equipped with storage, reading lights and double-sided shelves.

8 The bunk chamber can be accessed from the stair through an opening high in the wall.

A band of awning windows on the back wall of the main cabin ensures the flow of fresh air through the space.

"green" prefab cabin

DESIGN: RICHARD STARK, HY ROSENBERG AND TODD SAUNDERS, BLUESKY MOD

PHOTOGRAPHS: ELAINE KILBURN

LOCATION: ONTARIO, CANADA   416 SQUARE FEET

We all can identify with a cottage in the woods, but a *prefab* cottage in the woods? That might seem like a stretch of the imagination until we see the prototype cabin produced by a Toronto-based group of entrepreneurs who aim to change the way we think about the getaway house.

The company behind the concept is Bluesky Mod, a sunny name for what turns out to be a brilliant idea. Cofounded by Richard Stark, a custom residential builder, and Hy Rosenberg, a lawyer and businessman, the company has a tagline that is a bold but refreshing statement of its intent: "low-impact, high-design living." Says Stark, "It's about offering stylish living options that also happen to be eco-friendly. We wanted to show that sustainability and contemporary architectural aesthetics do not have to be mutually incompatible."

Designed by Canadian-born architect Todd Saunders, who now lives in Norway, the prototype shown in these pages reveals why prefabrication has become the buzzword in residential construction. The developers devised a system that makes it possible to fabricate and assemble the individual cabin components in a Toronto warehouse. The components can then be shipped in a kit for reassembly on the chosen site. No heavy equipment is required during reassembly; in fact, two people can raise the cabin in about fifteen days. As of this writing, the company was fine-tuning two other

SPECIAL FEATURES FOR THIS PLAN

- CAN BE PREASSEMBLED IN A WAREHOUSE AND THEN SHIPPED IN PIECES FOR ON-SITE REASSEMBLY
- INCORPORATES SUSTAINABLE AND RECYCLED MATERIALS AND LOW-WASTE BUILDING TECHNIQUES
- BUYER HAS THE OPTION OF CUSTOMIZING FLOOR PLANS, MATERIALS AND FINISHES

3

fabrication options: a cabin that can be shipped to the site as a fully constructed unit, and a more flexible kit that will allow the buyer to build the cabin on his preferred time line and using his own selection of materials.

"We're trying to achieve a balance between good design, function and sustainability," Stark says. "We want to make the process simple and accessible for people so they can modify the structure, adapt it to their needs, go to their site and put it together. We describe it as one-stop cabin shopping."

The prototype has little impact on the land and features local and recycled materials throughout. It sits on concrete piers (as an alternative, it can be placed on a concrete slab) and consists of two modules linked by an uncovered breezeway. The 288-square-foot main module combines a living area with a bedroom. A short walk down the breezeway takes the occupant to a 128-square-foot cabana equipped with a wood-burning sauna and a bathroom with a shower and composting toilet.

In keeping with the environmentally sound theme, the interior walls are finished with a formaldehyde-free wheat fiber compressed board, which is made from sustainable materials and comparable in cost to drywall. The home's energy-efficient double-glazed sliding

doors were crafted from cedar, a fast-growing and thus renewable resource, and the main cabin is heated with a Danish wood-burning stove that can be rotated to direct heat where it's needed.

Stark acknowledges that the cabin's ample glazing probably makes it more suited to a rural setting than a town street, but he points out that the retreat could be adapted for urban use—if the owner isn't a stickler for privacy. After all, city dwellers also dream of cozy cottages, even if they're not hidden in the woods.

1 The cabin's high-end detailing reveals that quality isn't reserved for custom one-of-a-kind architecture.

2 The cabin sits close to the ground on concrete piers and is bordered on three sides by a deck. The main living/ sleeping cabin in front is connected to the cabana/washroom by an exposed breezeway; the architect left the breezeway open to the elements to encourage the occupants to step outside on a regular basis, rain or shine. Cedar siding is renewable and, thus, sustainable, and high-density siding panels by Prodema are a cost-effective and eco-friendly choice.

3 The architect continued the ceiling material on the soffit, a popular technique for visually connecting indoor and outdoor spaces.

INTO THE FUTURE

202 "GREEN" PREFAB CABIN

5 Although diminutive in size, the cabana can accommodate a cedar-lined wood-burning sauna.

6 The cabana module has a composting toilet, small sink, shower/changing room and wood-burning sauna. The walls here and in the main cabin are finished with formaldehyde-free pre-stained compressed board made from wheat fiber.

7   The architect brought a uniform look to the exterior by using only one material—locally grown cedar—on the deck, soffit and roof fascia, and as siding. Tall double-glazed sliding doors on three sides of the cabin allow sunlight to penetrate the back wall and warm the interior.

8   The bedroom floor was finished in recycled off-cuts of engineered wood, which is durable, easy to repair if necessary and can be oiled to a deep sheen. Better yet, the material poses no risk of toxic offgassing and is comparable in cost to red oak hardwood. The ceiling is cedar.

9   Even the furniture in the main cabin is environmentally sound. The credenza frame was crafted from elm trees cut down during streetscape maintenance in downtown Toronto and the drawers are recycled reed veneer.

resources

ARCHITECTS & DESIGNERS

Matthew Ackerman
Catalyst Architecture
123 E. Goodwin Street
Prescott, AZ 86303
(928) 778-3508
www.catalystarchitecture.com

Kevin Burke
Carney Architects
P.O. Box 9218
215 South King Street
Jackson, WY 83002
(307) 733-4000
www.carneyarchitects.com

Richard Cieciuch
ProjectWorkshop
780 Pine Drive
Ridgway, CO 81432
(970) 626-5063
www.project-workshop.com

Eric Cobb
E. Cobb Architects, Inc.
911 Western Avenue, Suite 318
Seattle, WA 98104
(206) 287-0136
www.cobbarch.com

Elizabeth Danze
John Blood
Danze & Blood Architects
4701 Spicewood Springs Road
Austin, TX 78759
(512) 345-2320

Stephen Dynia
Stephen Dynia Architects
P.O. Box 4356
1135 Maple Way
Jackson, WY 83001
(307) 733-3766
www.dynia.com

Nathan Good
1586 Aloha Court
Salem, OR 97302
(503) 370-4448
www.nathangoodarchitect.com

Gar Hargens
Close Associates Architects
3101 E. Franklin Avenue
Minneapolis, MN 55406
(612) 339-0979

Jay Hargrave
Cottam Hargrave
701a S. Lamar
Austin, TX 78704
(512) 225-2400
www.cottamhargrave.com

Fred Herring
Herring & Worley, Inc.
1741 Broadway
Redwood City, CA 94063
(650) 361-1441
www.herringandworley.com

John Klopf
Klopf Architecture
3012–16th Street, Suite 206

San Francisco, CA 94103
(415) 283-5203
www.klopfarchitecture.com

Eric Logan
P.O. Box 9218
215 South King Street
Jackson, WY 83002
(307) 733-4000

Ron Mason
Anderson Mason Dale Architects
1615 Seventeenth Street
Denver, CO 80202
(303) 294-9448
www.amdarchitects.com

Dan Molenaar
Mafco House
309 Queen Street West
Toronto, Ontario, Canada M5V 2A4
(416) 985-0597
www.mafcohouse.com

Hy Rosenberg
Richard Stark
Bluesky Mod
(416) 694-3475
www.blueskymod.com

Michael Taylor
Taylor Smyth Architects
354 Davenport Road, Suite 3B
Toronto, Ontario, Canada M5R 1K6
(416) 968-6688
www.taylorsmyth.com

Patrick Tighe
Tighe Architecture, Inc.
1632 Ocean Park Boulevard
Santa Monica, CA 90405
(310) 450-8823
www.tighearchitecture.com

Candace Tillotson-Miller
P.O. Box 470
Livingston, MT 59047
(406) 222-7057
www.ctmarchitects.com

Charles Travis
CHAS Architects
1209 West 5th
Austin, TX 78703
(512) 476-1007
www.chasarchitects.com

Todd Walker
Archimania
356 South Main Street
Memphis, TN 38103
(901) 527-3560
www.archimania.com

David Webber
Webber Hanzlik Architects
Webber + Studio, Inc.
300 West Avenue, Suite 1322
Austin, TX 78701
(512) 236-1032
www.webberhanzlik.com

PHOTOGRAPHERS

Bernard André
Bernard André Photography
12 Medway Road
Woodside, CA 94062
(650) 400-5129
www.bernardandre.com

Paul Bardagjy
c/o Through the Lens
Management, Inc.
P.O. Box 2134
Wimberley, TX 78676-2134
(512) 847-7506
www.ttlmgt.com

Gerry Efinger
P.O. Box 259
Placerville, CO 81430
(970) 369-4894
www.newimagesphotography.com

Joseph Franke
(416) 598-0013

Christie Goss
P.O. Box 7354
Jackson, WY 83002

Art Gray
171 Pier Avenue, #272
Santa Monica, CA 90405
(310) 450-2806
www.artgrayphotography.com

Ken Gutmaker
5 Winfield Street
San Francisco, CA 94110
(415) 282-2600
www.kengutmaker.com

Greg Hursley
c/o Through the Lens
Management, Inc.
P.O. Box 2134
Wimberley, TX 78676
(512) 847-7506
www.ttlmgt.com

Steve Keating
Steve Keating Photography
5396 East Blaisdell Lane
Port Orchard, WA 98366
(206) 227-5878
www.steve-keating.com

Elaine Kilburn
Elaine Kilburn Photography
1-42 Kenneth Avenue
Toronto, Ontario, Canada M6P 1H9
(416) 766-4463
www.elainekilburn.com

Greg Kozawa
1801 NW Upshur, Suite 570
Portland, OR 97209
(503) 224-9300

Maxwell MacKenzie
2641 Garfield Street NW
Washington, D.C. 20008
(202) 232-6686
www.maxwellmackenzie.com

Cameron Neilson
The Seen Photography
P.O. Box 8485
Jackson, WY 83002
(307) 734-9775
www.theseenphoto.com

Ben Rahn
A-Frame Incorporated
9 Davies Avenue, Suite 303
Toronto, Ontario, Canada M4M 2A6
(416) 465-2426
232 Third Street
Brooklyn, NY 11215
(718) 875-9604
www.aframestudio.com

Roger Wade
Roger Wade Studio
79305 Highway 83
Swan Lake, MT 59911
(800) 507-6437
www.rogerwadestudio.com

Christopher Wadsworth
(416) 832-9068
www.closer-to-truth.com

Paul Warchol
Paul Warchol Photography
224 Centre Street, 5th Floor
New York, NY 10013
(212) 431-3461
www.warcholphotography.com

Don Wong
Don Wong Photo
8919 Vincent Place
Bloomington, MN 55431
(952) 948-9696
www.donwongphoto.com

Patrick Wong
Atelier Wong Photography
1009 East 40th Street, Suite 100
Austin, TX 78751
(512) 371-1288
www.atelierwong.com

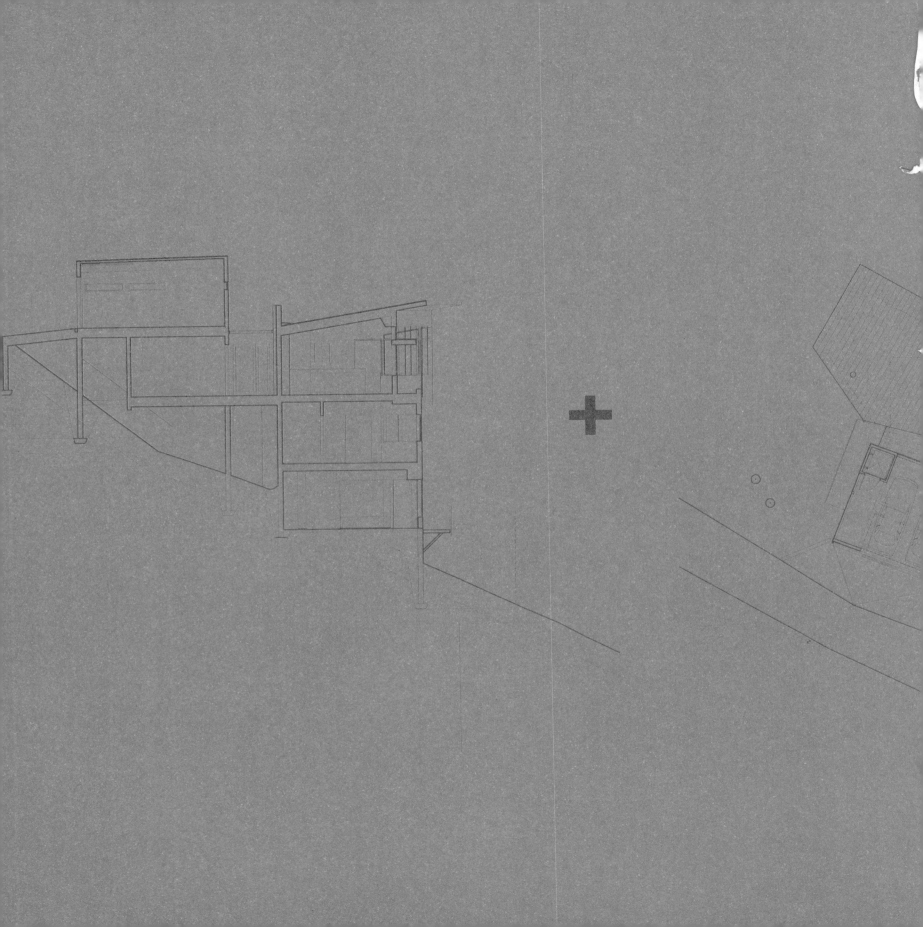